MARRIAGE

—

THE GREAT ADVENTURE

A CATHOLIC COUPLE'S GUIDE TO

LASTING LOVE

LINAS & RIMA SIDRYS

FOREWORD

My parents' story is one that has captivated my heart since I was old enough to understand it. My father and mother met and fell in love dancing, and they continue to dance through their lives with such grace and romance. As you'll come to find in the pages you are about to read, there is a delicate balance of that same feminine and masculine energy they exude on the dance floor.

My father took the lead: writing anytime he had the chance, which was typically in the middle of the night after long days at work. He challenges readers to stretch their intellect, strengthen their will, and fearlessly open their hearts. My mother adds a personal touch: connecting with readers, inspiring them to new heights and letting them know what wonders are possible for a marriage centered on God.

When my parents asked me to edit their book, I was at once surprised and honored. It wasn't just grammar and formatting they wanted me to check. They wanted me to address the most pressing needs of my generation: a generation facing rather difficult dating situations and paralyzing fears when it comes to marriage. Many of my friends grew up in broken homes. Years later, they talk about the scars that have persisted, even into adulthood.

My seven older siblings and I experienced a beautiful childhood as a result of the happy marriage we had at home. Even my brother, a Marine officer, admits that growing up in our family was nothing short of a fairytale.

However, it isn't fairies or magic you'll find in this tale; my parents aren't just "lucky" or simply "compatible." They really work at their relationship, they let their faith guide them, and they protect their marriage with the understanding that it is something sacred.

As one of their children, I can attest to the strength of their relationship. I'm a firsthand witness who can say, "It's true. What they've written on paper, they've lived out in real life—and it's worth emulating."

I am filled with such gratitude that my parents are generously sharing their parental love with those outside our home. I was able to see what an impact my parents' book made in Lithuania when we met overseas for their 2016 book tour. My father's wit had people roaring with laughter, while my mother's encouraging words moved them to tears.

This book will surely do incredible things near and far, far away: setting each reader on a path to their own great adventure.

With much love,
Žiba
The Youngest of Eight

TABLE OF CONTENTS

THE SEARCH FOR LASTING LOVE

"Each marriage is a kind of "salvation history," which from fragile beginnings – thanks to God's gift and a creative and generous response on our part – grows over time into something precious and enduring." - Pope Francis, Amoris Laetitia (The Joy of Love)

We decided to write about how to create a happy marriage and family. Even before saying our vows, we saw marriage as a great adventure we were about to embark upon; one that would bring on many difficulties and hurdles. We knew our love would be tested over and over again, but with God as our center we were not afraid.

These days we see many marriages suffering. Couples turning on each other, marriages ending in divorce, and homes torn apart. As a result, we have an entire generation that is skeptical about, or afraid of marriage. Our hope is that this book will not only give insights into the meaning of marriage but will also inspire you to see that marriage is not an impossible dream or mere drudgery, but a beautiful, lasting journey that you take with your spouse and family.

Keep in mind, we are not "experts"—after all, who is a marriage expert? We are a happily married, hard-working couple; parents of eight truly awesome grown children; and grandparents of sixteen gregarious grandchildren. We also taught marriage preparation courses for twelve years in the Chicagoland area. This book explains how we lived out our marriage, how it shaped our family culture, and how we share that joy with others.

Does any couple really have a lot of "wisdom" to share with others? If they do, why are there so few books on marriage written by happily married couples? So many romantic movies, but so much confusion! We think some couples want to write down thoughts about their marriage, but don't find the time; or, they are too modest or shy. Most likely, they start arguing and can't finish chapter two! Melinda Gates writes in her book, "The Moment of Lift:" "The first time Bill and I sat down to write our Annual Letter together, I thought we were going to kill each other..."

It wasn't easy, but Rima and I have survived the ordeal of co-authorship. We were determined to write down points that we live by because we believe that Catholic teachings on marriage, both demanding and lofty, are not only livable—they are lovable! They truly are the key to keeping the romance alive. They allow couples to aim for the highest ideals and then learn to love one another more when they inevitably fall short, as we all do.

This book examines the search for, and secrets of a lasting love in marriage. We know that sadly many people these days do not even believe real happiness can be found or can last. But it can. It will require adjustments to immature behavior and adolescent dreams. Love in marriage is not just an emotional and physical bond; it is a spiritual journey: one that requires thought, willpower and endurance.

Love also requires a leap of faith. We jump into our lover's arms with the expectation that the other will catch us and hold on to us. This takes Faith, Hope and Love!

All storybooks end with "They lived happily..." But how did they do it? What did they do after they got married? We want to know more!

We hope this book maps out some answers. Whether you are a person of faith, or still searching, what you'll need is an open mind and an adventurous spirit. If you accept this challenge, let's begin.

RIMA'S STORY

My story begins in the south side of Chicago where I grew up in a Lithuanian family and bi-cultural community. Both of my parents were refugees who survived World War II. They instilled in me and my three older siblings a love of our Lithuanian heritage and a love of freedom in America. We were accustomed to looking at things differently, and in fact, we *were* different; everything from speaking a different language to attending Lithuanian Saturday school.

This constant evaluation and comparison of cultures, made me intellectually curious about the world of ideas and led me to the study of Philosophy at the University of Illinois, Chicago. Even though I grew up Catholic, I was agnostic in my early teens, and in college I became an avid atheist. After four years of atheistic philosophies: particularly existentialism, nihilism and relativism, I was confused and depressed. I found that the philosophers could neither prove the existence of God, nor could they prove that he does not exist. Descartes, the Father of Modern Philosophy famously said, "I think, therefore, I am." Like him, at the end of all my studies, I derived my own formula about reality: "If anything is possible, so is God."

After this insight, I began my new personal quest to find truth. I decided to give Christianity another look. After I graduated, I read the Bible, cover to cover. Some explanation was needed, and so my sister, a Jehovah's Witness, was happy to oblige. After a year of studying the Bible with her, she pressed me to make a decision for God and to join her congregation. I still had serious doubts about their interpretation of the Bible, particularly about the authority of Peter. However, I was miserable. I was "neither hot, nor cold—but lukewarm" about God. One evening, I became so disturbed about not knowing which of the many Christian churches was the true one, that I got down on my knees and prayed from the bottom of my (agnostic) heart. I said, "God, I am not sure you exist, but if you do, please reveal yourself and your true Church to me as soon as possible; I cannot bear to live with uncertainty a day longer!" In the back of my mind I was also saying: "Please God, not the Catholic Church."

A day or two later, I got my answer. I didn't know it was the answer right away. I was invited by an old family friend to return to the Lithuanian Folk Dance group in Chicago. They needed experienced dancers for the upcoming Folk Dance Festival. She wanted me to meet this "upstanding medical student from a very good family." I told her I was not interested in joining the group after already having danced for eight years. Besides, I had no way of getting there. She insisted I come anyway and said someone would pick me up.

When I went to the practice, the dancers were new and too inexperienced for me, and the young man didn't even show up. I decided I would definitely not be coming back. The following week, the same dance teacher called again, and arranged a ride. After some discussion, I relented.

That is how I became a dance partner to my future husband, who was the "answer" to my plea to God. He was not only a serious, practicing Catholic—he seemed to have all the answers to all of my questions and doubts about the Catholic faith. He was very well-informed and well-formed in his faith. It also helped that he was handsome, intellectual, talented and a Lithuanian-American like me. Still, I had my doubts if we were a good match.

We dated for some time, and we used to go for nature walks. We talked a lot about life, philosophy and faith. On several occasions, he suggested that we should walk in silence for awhile. I thought this was very deep and romantic, so finally one time I asked, "I feel so peaceful when we walk in silence, but I am curious about what you are doing or thinking about during those 20 minutes? Are you meditating?" Without a word, with simplicity and charm, he pulled a Rosary out of his pocket and showed it to me.

Immediately I understood that he had been praying for me, for us! I was flooded with such light and warmth, that I said to myself, "I want a faith just like that!" In that instant, all of my doubts disappeared, and my love for this man was confirmed. At the same time, my love for Our Lady and for the Church was enkindled. Ever since that day, I have never looked back.

LINAS' STORY

I was born in New York City to two European physicians. They were rootless and penniless, but very educated and cultured refugees from Communist-occupied Lithuania. Their trials made them a strong and loving couple.

My family moved from New York to Illinois, and then to the Philippine Islands so that my father could practice as a physician at Clark Air Force Base. The military chaplains taught me much about my Catholic faith, in the classroom and by their good example. Even in grade school, I noted the happy family lives of the devout Filipino Catholics and the many young Irish-American families on base. It was obvious to me that the Catholic faith was the basic thread that connected these Europeans, Americans and Asians in a special way. Like most other families in the community, my family went to Sunday Mass together and to the donut breakfasts that followed, but we were not overly pious.

At my undergraduate years at the University of Notre Dame, the official emphasis was on forming a caring "Christian community." The statue of Mary on top of the golden dome of the administration building could be seen from the entire campus, and that left an impression on me. Notre Dame means "Our Lady" in French, and with that statue it felt like she could see us; she was our Mother too. With a "just do it" hippie mentality, widespread drug use and violent anti-war, anti-establishment protests spreading across campuses nationwide, I knew that divine grace and Mary's intercession was especially needed. I began praying more, for my family, country, and for my future spouse. I started to attend daily Mass in the dorm. I was pre-med, but also took many excellent philosophy and political science courses.

At my medical school and residency programs at the University of Chicago, "the life of the mind" was the ideal. The mind, apparently, does not need football nor fun because the student motto was, "U of C—the place where fun goes to die," and that wasn't too far off. The university encouraged students to read the Great Books series, compiled by Mortimer Adler, and to critique all preconceived notions, especially those based on religion. The medical school seemed to subscribe to "teaching by terrorism," and pushed sleep-deprived students to their limits. I focused intently on medicine and ophthalmology but knew that faith and family were also important in my future.

My corneal surgery fellowship year was at the University of Florida, Gainesville. The medical personnel were totally isolated from the fun-loving, sun-centered, relaxed Floridian culture around us. We were in a very different, very driven world than the other students on campus. I was grateful for the excellent education from dedicated eye surgeons. I learned to transplant living corneas, implant plastic lenses, repair eye trauma, fight exotic eye infections and corneal ulcers, and teach eager young Residents.

However, it wasn't in the classroom or the lab that I found the love of my life—rather, it was in a Chicago Lithuanian Folk Dance group. I suspected behind-the-scenes matchmaking, but what can I say, it worked! The young lady, Rima, was presented to be my partner, and indeed was the best dancer in the group. Her vivacious smile, elegance and intelligent conversations caught my attention immediately. Dancing, chess games, cultural outings and intellectual discussions quickly drew us together. Even though she was not a practicing Catholic at the time, I could see that she was searching for something and eager to learn more.

SECTION I

SEXUAL ATTRACTION

When I first met my husband to be, I found him attractive in every way. He was tall, dark and handsome, with a deep voice that gave me butterflies. I cannot say, however, that he was immediately irresistible to me. He wasn't the typical "dream guy" I had in mind. I purposely avoided medical students. I was turned off by that fantasy of typical Lithuanian mothers that their daughters marry rich doctors, and by my own idea that doctors were superior, driven and not very romantic. I imagined I would marry some philosophy professor, or an artistic type, perhaps an architect, and we would live a creative, bohemian lifestyle together. That was my fantasy.

If I had met Linas even a year or two before I actually did, I would not have appreciated the kind of person that he was. Besides, I did not think I was his type: I was not a practicing Catholic at the time we met, not as academically ambitious, having only a bachelor's degree, somewhat alienated from the Lithuanian community which meant so much to him, and I had a very animated personality, in contrast to his silent reserve.

Those differences didn't seem to bother Linas in the slightest. He could have had any girl he wanted… Nevertheless, he was persistent in showing his interest and attraction to me. I noticed right away that his approach was very different than other guys at the time—who tended to be superficial. Moreover, he always treated me like a lady, which not only made me trust him, but it made me see him as very manly and romantic.

The two of us connected on a cultural and intellectual level, as well as physical: we were definitely attracted to one another. We were always affectionate with one another: with tender kisses, hugs, gazing into each other's eyes, holding hands, exchanging sweet words and writing letters to one another. However, we never took the physical affection too far: we kept it chaste before marriage. We avoided situations which would make it hard for us to resist each other. I am forever grateful to Linas who kept it that way due to his being a genuine Catholic gentleman.

IN LOVE WITH LOVE

"Genuine Love is demanding. But its beauty lies precisely in the demands it makes." - Pope John Paul II

If you take a look at any movie made or book written, romantic love is almost always incorporated there somehow. It can be the most gruesome film packed with murder, mystery and gore, but somewhere in the plot a love story is sure to creep in. This is because, whether we admit it or not, we are all in love with love. And it makes sense! It makes sense because we are all made by a God who *is* Love, and we are created *for* Love. Deep down in all of our hearts is an insatiable yearning to be seen, known and loved forever.

Without God in our lives, however, we try to have all the longings of our heart met by another person. From childhood, we see false ideas of love reinforced over and over again by our culture. Even in Disney movies such as *The Little Mermaid*, the mermaid sees a man on a ship: instantly "falling in love." Later his ship sinks and she is left with a sunken stone statue of the sailor.

In real life, some couples fall in love like this—quickly, and with no other concern but their feelings. Later, the young lady might realize she's stuck with a young man with a heart of stone; immature, irresponsible and unwilling to change. Sadly, that's the end of the love story in many people's lives. They don't experience the "happily ever after" that Disney stories promise.

We need to go back and begin at that moment when the mermaid sees the sailor. She's attracted and drawn to him, which is a very good thing. She might have found someone who she can love and who can love her in return. God instilled in her a desire for that man.

But instead of dwelling on a fantasy, she needs to ask the vital questions, do the "research" and start some soul-searching.

When we consider marriage, we must put away childish things. "When I was a child, I spake as a child, I understood as a child, I thought as a child: but when I became a man, I put away childish things." Cor. 13:11.

We often have an ideal of a perfect person for us, but then we are not really loving the person as they truly are, with their strengths and their faults. Romantic love should not ignore reality. It is getting to know the real person, taking the time to unlock the mystery of the other and preparing for the eventual giving of oneself through sexual love.

This gradual discovery of one another on every level is far more exciting than a childhood fairytale or a one-night stand. Instead of being left with disillusionment and bitterness, you open the door to a more demanding, but much more meaningful relationship.

True love transforms us. The Lord says: "I will take away your heart of stone and give you a heart of flesh." Ezekiel 36:22.

WHEN HORMONES TAKE OVER

"Some love with the selfish, capricious and self-centered love of a child: an insatiable love that screams or cries when it fails to get what it wants." - Pope Francis, Amoris Laetitia (The Joy of Love)

Once we grow out of fairytale stories, our idea of love shifts once again. As we mature, we become more aware of our physical bodies and the differences in masculinity and femininity. The excitement of it all, mixed with the rush of new hormones, however, makes it hard to differentiate between lust and love.

It's like those summer days on the beach as teens. The girls are hoping to get noticed in their tiny bikinis. Their new curves are barely covered by tiny cloth tied with string. The boys all watch closely, hoping to see more, but the bikinis don't wash off in the waves.

This "summer loving" is actually lust—but try telling that to a teenage boy. It's very hard to reason with a hormone-charged brain. The logic is irrational. It is totally emotional. If adults try to explain why sexual intimacy outside of marriage is wrong, teens won't listen. Their answer: "It's my body! I can do what I want!" or, "You don't understand, I'm in love!"

This should make us all stop and think, when, exactly, did your body become "yours?" Your parents, together with God, created your body. What you must realize is that you actually have a "caretaker" relationship to your body, not "ownership." That means you will have to give an account to God of how well you took care of your body in this life, and what you did with it.

If it's "your body," can you make yourself taller? "Which of you... can add one cubit to your height?" Luke 12:25. No, you can't add to your height. You can only add to your weight… which we're all unfortunately too good at.

By giving in to sex outside of marriage, you're actually harming the person you think you love. You are depriving that person of the opportunity to mature, to grow spiritually, to learn and to develop a spiritual life. You are preventing that person, and yourself, from becoming "the best version of him or herself," as the famous Catholic speaker Matthew Kelly would say.

You show your beloved real love by saying "no" to a false commitment outside of marriage. Your decision to go in, shut the bedroom door and turn off the lights, will shut the door and leave you in the dark on something much better.

This self-control needs to be realized early in life. Human virtues must be developed at home, such as temperance, patience and purity. We all must learn to wait, not to get what we want right when we want it. Teenagers need to develop more self-esteem and confidence in their self-worth, to deal with peer-pressure and to resist the prevailing sexualized social mores.

When sleeping around, you become just a body "in the dark," a body easily exchanged for someone else. You will be kicked out of that bed, sooner or later. The immoral universe is heartless, opportunistic and sadly unstable, because everyone is only looking out for themselves.

The secular view states that the sexual hormonal drive is so strong it cannot, and should not, ever be denied or controlled. In fact, some have the opinion that self-control is unhealthy, that there must always be physical release. This view is very self-centered and totally false. There is a difference between being in control of your sexuality and suppressing it. As Catholics, we seek to control our sexual urges, so that they don't enslave and control us. Building up this strength is essential in order to stay faithful when temptations arise. It means restricting your show of physical affection while dating (to kissing, caressing…), so that it's appropriate to your level of commitment to that other person.

Physical intimacy is an expression of love. It is telling another person you want to come together and be one with them forever—so much so that you want to bear another life, together. This is a commitment which only makes sense, and is only true, within marriage. In any other instance, this is a lie being told by your bodies. No relationship should ever begin with a lie—especially one as important as marriage. It is the truth you should seek together with your spouse, for as long as you both shall live.

The fact that sex outside of marriage is bad does not mean that the human body, and physical love itself is bad. American society is quite confused about this. They are either too prudish or too obsessed with the naked body and sex.

Catholics are not prudish nor obsessed with sex. We know that God created the human body to be incredibly beautiful and attractive. In Catholic cultures the human form is celebrated in art and sculpture, in churches and public square fountains. Men and women can look at a masterpiece painting of a nude woman or man, delight in the beauty of its form and avoid any trace of impurity. However, in everyday life we should, of course, dress with reasonable modesty, because we want to draw attention to our personalities more than our bodies.

Protestants, especially Puritans, mistakenly thought the physical body itself was sinful, not to be looked at. They even removed the naked body of Christ from the crucifix. Catholics, however, are not afraid to gaze upon the body of Christ, who gave himself up on a cross for love of us.

Our bodies are also made to express our love for our spouse. In marriage, we gaze upon each other with a pure love. The beauty of the masculine and feminine form reveals itself fully in the passionate marital embrace.

IS IT ALL ABOUT CHEMISTRY?

"Sexuality is not a means of gratification or entertainment; it is an interpersonal language wherein the other is taken seriously, in his or her sacred and inviolable dignity." - Pope Francis, Amoris Laetitia (Joy of Love)

Moving on to college can present a whole array of issues when it comes to learning about love. As we've said before, and will state over and over again—God is Love, so leaving Him at home with the parents or parish church when headed to college is an unfortunate step that students often take. Half of Catholics 30 years old and younger have left the church.[1] They think religion is irrelevant in their lives. This group has become what is commonly known as the "nones."

In place of faith, students are taught that the scientific method is the only reliable way to determine what is real. Only things that can be measured and quantified are to be considered real. Thus, theology and classical philosophy are not taught. The philosophers are mentioned only as historical figures. Philosophy courses are existentialist, atheist, nihilist or reduced to the mere study of words. The mention of the Bible, even as a literary or historic document, is banned from the classroom. The sense of the sacred has been eliminated from our secular culture and also from our understanding of true love.

This restriction of real knowledge to the sciences has a profound impact on us. We no longer know where we came from or where we are going. Our sense of worth is diminished. The standards for art and beauty cannot be distinguished from violence or pornography. Students cannot talk about morality, because according to their

---

[1] Arch Bishop Barron, Robert. Catholic News Service: 12 June 2019.

teachers, there is no objective right or wrong. They do not think about virtues, because virtues have been replaced by "values." These values are purely subjective evaluations, divorced from the moral teachings of revelation and the classical philosophers.

Discussion of ethical decisions are now based on political correctness. Moral judgements have shifted away from Jesus' transcendent teachings: "I am the way, the truth and the life…" John 14:6, to the attitude of Pontius Pilate: "What is Truth?". Thus your truth is not my truth, because there is no objective truth. This mindset is what we call moral relativism, and it is now the norm in today's education.

To make matters worse, peer-pressure for premarital sexual activity is immense. Sexual exploration of all types is encouraged at a young age, because "everyone is doing it."

Two of the best-known speakers to youth on the subject of chastity and resisting "peer pressure" to have pre-marital sex are Jason and Crystalina Evert. In "Pure Manhood" Jason writes, "With chastity, you're able to rise above the urge of your hormones, the invitations of the Internet, the ridicule of your peers, the pressure of a date, or the enticement of an affair in marriage. With chastity, none of these things has control over you, and you are free to love." He also presents the following concept which gives hope to everyone. "Even if you've already lost your virginity, you can still choose to start over and live the virtue of purity. Regardless, of the past, it's never too late to become the man (or woman) you ought to be."

Many women think sexual favors are the only way to attract and keep a man. But the anxiety of trying to keep a man's attention in this hyper-sexualized world makes dating more stressful than enjoyable. Ask any single young woman, and she'll likely have stories and emotional scars to prove it.

Young people thus face a problem when it comes to love. This attraction feels "real." But how does one really know, as there is no objective measurement of love. Does love even exist? Is this infatuation just hormonal? Do we have the right "chemistry" to make a commitment? How do we make it last? Why wasn't this topic ever covered in Chemistry class?

We need to test this scientifically. We need to do a trial run, and maybe a comparison test with other people. We need to spend many nights together. The intimacy and exchange of bodily fluids is an obvious and objective indicator of compatibility, right? Will the sparks fly? Will we rub each other the wrong way? Will I feel better when I get what I want? What, and how much, does the other person expect or demand? Are they being unreasonable or am I? Too emotional? Too possessive? Too flakey?

So much uncertainty, so much anxiety already! If these are the types of questions being asked, the predicted outcome is that the two will not respect one another and things will take a turn for the worse. They're making the other person out to be an object of use, and the questions are regarding that person's usefulness. The body of the other becomes an object of curiosity for personal use and self-satisfaction. No matter how much we "love" objects, we do not respect them the same way we respect a human person—full of dignity and worth.

Love is not a bunch of chemicals, wrestling matches, comparisons and evaluations. Leave the experiments to rats in a lab. Real Love is poetry, not to be found in a test tube. When love is real, the "unknown" element in the chemistry experiment will remain unknown, and the mystery will last.

The love of God is this great unknown. There is no real or lasting love without God in the mix. When God is found in the middle of your relationship, there is an underlying excitement that will be there in all of your daily interactions. In marriage you will find a sense of sacredness and mystery in physical intimacy. Its strength will create a spiritual bond between you and your spouse.

SEX IS A GIFT FROM GOD

"When a young man or woman recognizes that authentic love is a precious treasure, they are also enabled to live their sexuality in accordance with the divine plan." - Pope John Paul II

So far, we've learned what happens to love and sex when they're reduced to fantasy or to a matter of mere hormones and sexual compatibility. We invite you to see sex in a radically new way.

In the past, sex, even in marriage, was thought to be somewhat shameful, very embarrassing, a "necessary evil," and certainly not a fitting subject for theological analysis. In those days, the common view was that a young man "got" a woman who obeyed the "master" of the house, "met his needs," produced babies and raised his children. Sadly, this view was true in society at large as well as in the church, but it was totally wrong.

Fortunately for all of us, the charismatic Pope John Paul II gave a series of weekly talks called, "Theology of the Body," which explained the sexual union in a radically new way. The sexual act has a specific spirituality: with more depth, more bonding and more radical equality, than we had realized. John Paul II called it the "Spousal meaning of the body," because the human body expresses the love in which each person becomes a gift to the other.

Rima and I refer to the broader spirituality of the marriage bond as, "Nuptial Spirituality." This spirituality is an integral part of your everyday married life. It assumes this new, correct understanding of the nuptial bond and the physical, sexual union. It is a "reciprocal gift of oneself."

Each person is a unity of body and soul. Our body and soul are so tightly bound that our sexuality cannot be separated from our person. The body *is* personal. One of the most basic and foundational truths is that all humans image God individually, as each person is made in the "image and likeness of God."[2]

Pope John Paul II elaborates even further and says humans also reveal their likeness to God as a married couple. They make visible the invisible reality of God—that He is Love—total, unselfish and generous. The human body expresses this Love in the physical act in which the human person becomes a gift to the other. Thus the sexual act should be an act of total self-giving, not just a physical union.

Your body and soul are given to you by God so that you can give them away. This is what Pope John Paul II means when he says; "Man can fully discover his true self only in a sincere giving of himself."[3] The appropriate reaction to this is: Wow! It is not what a person *gets*, but what they *give*—in all areas of life—that make life worth living. You can see that this idea was, and still is, very counter-cultural. Our society continuously tells us to *get* as much as we can.

The amazing beauty of the human body was made for love. The surprising papal letter, "Deus Caritas Est" (God is Love) also examines eros (erotic) and agape (unconditional) love. Pope Benedict's conclusion: "the powerful dynamic of desire—eros—is itself a sign that souls are made for and directed to a love which never ends—agape."

When a married couple are making love, they are in a metaphysical way, re-expressing their marriage vows. It is an authentic sign of their deep, personal and permanent allegiance to each other. They give the seed of their very selves. Man acts quintessentially as man, and the woman quintessentially as woman.

---

[2] Gen. 1:26 NKJV.

[3] General Audience of Wednesday, 26 Aug. 1998.

Each have a unique role, and so they cannot fulfill the full power and purpose of sex without the other.[4]

Together, a man and woman possess the power to "be fruitful and multiply."[5] Each person only has half the generative power. In sex, they are giving their generative power to each other. Take a moment to think about that. There is nothing more powerful than the ability to generate new life—an entirely new, equal and eternal being. When you make love with your spouse, you are giving your strongest power, your greatest gift to them and them alone.

So the first purpose of sex is to recapitulate the marriage vows: strengthen that personal allegiance to one another by bonding with one another. This bond is necessary—so necessary it is intrinsic to the act. Why is that so? Why are such strong bonding hormones and emotions released during the sexual act? Because, we need a bond that will last for years, for a lifetime. A new life will depend on it.

Pro-creation quite naturally begets new life, in the creation of a child. This is the second gift and essential purpose of sex according to "Theology of the Body." This second purpose of marriage is inseparable from the first. Total self-giving means you and your spouse are both open to the possibility of new life flowing from the sexual act. It is the classical teaching of the Church that each sexual act is *unitive* and *procreative,* and these should not, and cannot, be separated.

Your spousal love, if open to life, will take you on a great new adventure—the *co-creation* of a new immortal soul. Each child is an invaluable gift that has been born out of your deep, personal and generous gift to your spouse, and to God.

---

[4] Newton, William. FOCUS: Fellowship of Catholic University Students. SLS Conference 2020: Talk given on Wednesday, 1 Jan. 2020.

[5] Gen. 1:28 NKJV.

MADE FOR MISSION

"The effectiveness and the success of their life – their happiness – depends to a great extent on their awareness of their specific mission." - St. Josemaria Escriva

St. Augustine, sixteen hundred years ago, noted that there exist two cities; the city of God, and the city of man.[6] Each person must decide where he will live, in the life of the spirit, or only in the physical world. As a young man, St. Augustine was a pagan philosopher and lived in the city of man: a life of pleasure without God. He fathered a child with the woman he was living with. He later converted to Christianity and was baptized together with his son. In St. Augustine's "Confessions," he reveals this great truth about ourselves: "You have made us for yourself, O Lord, and our heart is restless until it rests in you!" St. Augustine is a perfect example of "beginning again," with the grace of God.

We are body and spirit, and we cannot ignore either. If you were a body without a spirit you'd be a zombie. If you were a spirit without a body you'd be a ghost. There's a reason the two are reserved for horror films. Humans who try to live solely by the body lose something very special. What we do with our bodies greatly affects our souls.

If these issues are confused, we will lose our way and then our self-esteem. The older generation, parents and teachers, tried to teach their kids social morals and virtuous behavior, but they did not know how to inspire in them this spiritual dimension. Devoid of the divine, "correct" behavior is seen by the young as parental control,

---

[6] St. Augustine,; Marcus Dods, trans. "The City of God." (New York: Modern Library, 1950.)

hypocrisy and a reason to rebel. Loss of inner peace, anxiety and fear of commitment are traits of the times.

Thus, we all must develop a sense of our truth self-worth and self-confidence, to decide how we plan to live, and where we will live. The city of God, or somewhere else? To enter this city of God, we need to understand our great dignity as adopted "children of God." This is our spiritual birthright. We cannot love others if we don't love ourselves as the Creator loves us. How do we know that the Creator loves us? Well, He sent us His son to bridge the gap between fallen humanity and divine Father. Jesus has restored our relationship with God so that we can come to know Him and be more like Him.

All of us are called to a mission by Christ, but it's up to each one of us individually to answer the call. Our lives will look very different depending on how we respond.

Consider two high school friends. One is happily married with children. He wakes up in the morning next to his wife. He has the joyful conviction that he is a child of God: a God who is personally interested in his innermost being. He knows God calls him daily, in the little things of each day. He knows he is not his own master, but he depends on God. This dependency is not a sad thing—it is the relationship of a child to their Father. This God has adopted us into his family, so this man knows he is a son of God! He has his own family, but at the same time he knows he is living in God's extended family. God depends on him! This conviction is inspiring and exciting!

This man gets out of bed during the night to give a bottle to the baby, and in the morning, cereal to the kids. He knows these little acts of service that allow his wife to sleep, are of infinite value, because Christ said: "If you give even a cold cup of water to these little ones... you shall have your reward." Matt. 10:42. His family needs him, so he is striving to become a better husband, father, neighbor. He would give his life for his family!

Those who are not ready to die for someone, do not know why they are living. Religious faith gives us this inspiration and strength.

The second friend to consider, chose a different path. He wakes up hungover and groggy, in an existential fog. He has no belief in the spiritual. He thinks religious people are hypocrites. He hears no inner call, feels no mission in life, serves no one other than himself. He wants to be "free" and yet he is enslaved by his own vices and passions. His only objective is to please himself, look for entertainment and to feel good. He picks up girls, but avoids emotional commitments. He seeks instant gratification. He is surprised to find that most of the time he is quite bored. Even sex has become boring. His room is a mess and his social life a disaster. Most of his friends have started families and have stopped calling him. He feels somewhat empty, restless and depressed. He uses recreational drugs for relief, and the sad spiral downward has begun...

What is your mission? What is Christ asking of you? For most people it's the vocation of marriage. Not just to get married and to "settle down." That already sounds boring! Vocation means a calling. A calling from Christ should stir the soul and uproot one's life.

Building a life together with another human being and bringing new life into the world is a most incredible undertaking. You want to be sure you are ready and that you have the right person at your side when the time comes to get married and have children.

- - -

Consider this lovely statement from a married Christian writer, Quintus Tertulianus, in the early Church, around the year 200 AD:

"How can I ever express the happiness of a marriage joined by the Church, strengthened by an offering, sealed by a blessing, announced by angels, and ratified by the Father?... How wonderful the bond between two believers, now one in hope, one in desire, one in discipline, one in the same service! They are both children of one Father and servants of the same Master..."

The early Christians realized that sacramental marriages also involved the Father, the offering of the Son, and the blessings of the Holy Spirit. These communities slowly replaced the hedonistic Roman society, and formed the foundation of Western civilization.

SECTION II

MARRIAGE PREP

Linas and I met in a Lithuanian folk dance group. Just as we worked on each dance routine, we also worked out what we wanted of our friendship, of dating and eventually of marriage. While engaged, we read out loud, "Marriage, a Christian Vocation," from a book called, "Christ is Passing By" by St. Josemaria Escriva which really inspired us.

It gave us a higher purpose and a clear direction as a couple. Instead of just looking inward at one another, we were looking outward, at God's plan for us. Part of that plan meant maintaining a chaste relationship before marriage. If that seems negative or dull, like we were depriving ourselves of something, it was the exact opposite.

Saving physical intimacy for marriage opened up a whole new world of possibilities in our lives. It was both exciting and romantic. We were able to plan and dream about the future. We chose not to do whatever everyone else was doing, but rather, we set out to meet a challenge, an almost impossible one—which brought out the best in us.

We both were ready to start a family, even a large one, to create something new and incredible in the world. We were willing to take on the challenge put forth by St. Josemaria Escriva in his homily "Marriage, a Christian Vocation":

"A married couple should build their life together on the foundation of a sincere and pure affection for each other, and on the joy that comes from having brought into the world the children God has enabled them to have. They should be capable of renouncing their personal comfort; and they should put their trust in the providence of God."

We were dating for about a year when Linas surprised me with his wedding proposal. I really thought he was too ambitious in his medical career to start a family so soon. After all, he had just started his ophthalmology residency. I was thrilled that he was willing to take the risk, and so of course, I said yes!

- - -

Note the dynamic interaction of a couple dancing on stage. They are confidently doing their routine with an audience in awe of them. Every couple begins to dance, and eventually in marriage, they have their own routine. A good dance routine requires the correct discipline and dedication by both parties before they are paired up.

Once they meet, the couple is eager to begin. The man leads the woman out to the stage. They move together as one, and their passion lights up the stage. They anticipate the other's movements, emotions, need for support... Even when moving separately, each always knows where the other one is, where each is going, and when they will meet again.

The woman dazzles. She is gorgeous in her makeup, jewelry and sparkling clothes. Her beautiful figure says: "Look at me!" This is as it should be; a woman's curves are a work of art. The man's shoulders and legs are strong, made for supporting and lifting.

The romantic ingredients are all there: the music, the lights, the physical touch, the smiles. Their joy and enthusiasm of dancing together is evident, even though they must have practiced this routine hundreds of times. This routine took hours and hours of practice. They have defeated tedium, they have overcome pain, they have mastered friction, acceleration, momentum and gravity. They bring us hope and joy; if they can do it, we can do it in our own lives also!

If things don't go well that day, a dance partner never leaves their partner on stage alone. They stay together. They're a team in bad times and in good. There is always a chance to do better next time. They inspire more people than they know. A good couple can bring color, warmth and love of life to the cold world. So keep on dancing!

THE FOUR PILLARS OF MARRIAGE

Take a close look at marriages that are strong, dynamic and long-lasting. They are often based on solid principles, like the four legs of a table. When the "weight of life" comes down, this marriage has strong support. It holds up. But if a table has a weak leg, it will tilt, and things on the table may slide off. The table may even topple over...

Align your marriage supports before the weight of life (arguments, job stress, children, finances, extended family, health issues, and the burdens of routine) is placed on your table. Find couples that are truly happy, and have been married for at least 10 years. See if the following four supports are in place.

If couples do not try to reconcile important differences in these four areas before marriage, it will be much harder for them to reconcile after the vows. Before marriage there is a great desire to know the beloved, to discuss issues and to resolve problems. The betrothed are ready to open up their hearts to each other and to make changes. Here is a list of questions to ask yourselves.

FAITH

Most students neglect their faith in college, and are confused or swayed by the moral relativism they see on campus. But God is Love, so couples who truly love one another get an insight into Divine Love.

Do both share a similar religious faith? Do you have the same moral values, compatible world views, the same vision of where your family life should be headed? Do you communicate these values to each other? Do both of you want to live virtuous lives, or is someone living a life of dishonesty? Are you both mature enough to be able to give yourself as a "gift" to the other? Do you both answer to a higher power, worship God and pray regularly?

Do both of you see children as a positive good, a blessing from God, not just a checklist item or burden? Are you willing to be open to life as much as possible? Does your family support you in these decisions? If you are Catholic, do you rely on the sacraments of Confession and Communion to give you the graces for the supreme challenges of marriage and parenting? If you are not Catholic Christian, do you pray regularly? Do you have a faith support group?

We use the expression "supreme challenges of marriage and parenting" because almost everyone who gets married is eventually shocked to find out just how difficult and all-consuming marriage and parenting become. And then spouses must learn to balance all of this with professional work. Basically, you have to learn to multitask, be a juggler, become a child psychologist, all of it while severely sleep-deprived. It takes years of practice! Just when you learn to do it, the kids will leave the house and you will become "empty nesters": another difficult adjustment for the couple.

FAMILY & FRIENDS

Is there a similar upbringing, culture, level of education, ethnicity? Is there positive family support? Are there many divorces in the family? If so, what were the causes of the divorce? Are you ready to put in extra effort to make your own family function properly? Do your family and friends approve of your choice of spouse? Do you like each other's family and friends? Can you become good friends with them? Perhaps they are too "chummy" and demanding of your time? Are they too critical? Family means community; are you ready to be in this community?

Have you identified the differences in your strongly held personal opinions, and how to deal with that? Is there a sense of humor, but not at the other's expense? Is there respect for personal freedom? Is there a lot of eccentric behavior or emotional pressures? Do you both agree that in your marriage, the needs and desires of your spouse will come before all others, including your parents, siblings, best friends, and even your own children?

FITNESS

Are you both physically healthy? Are there any chronic diseases in your family history? Are there mental health issues such as depression or anxiety? What is the level of physical and emotional health, strength and stamina, commitment to healthy eating and regular exercise? Are you prepared to work harder, physically and mentally, at your marriage and parenting than anything else in your life?

Is anyone lazy or indifferent to self-improvement? Are there unhealthy habits or obsessions, harmful addictions of any kind: drugs, drinking, smoking, gambling, or pornography which is so pervasive today. If there are addictions, has there been any progress in controlling and resolving them, especially before marriage?

FINANCES

Are there similar standards of living and lifestyle? Could you live on one income if necessary? Can one of the parents stay home to raise the children? Are you both willing to make the financial sacrifice staying at home would require? Do you both recognize that being a homemaker is a profession? What happens if one spouse becomes ill or loses a job? Will there be financial freedom to live comfortably and to do things that are important or fun? Are one or both spouses frugal, too frugal, or spendthrifts? Will you consult with your spouse before spending over a certain limit? Do you have parents or family that are willing to help you with finances or child care, in tight situations?

Do you realize, that after love, the gospels write the most about finances, and strongly urge one to avoid debt? Christ praised people who made good use of their talents, earned money and were generous in donating to good causes.

Do you both agree on how money should be saved or spent? Do you both agree to share all things in common, including bank accounts, property, debt, etc? Do not underestimate the need to be in agreement on finances and where to spend or invest money, because most arguments and many divorces are about finances.

We all have heard the saying that "opposites attract." However, in reality, it is often easier to make a life together with someone you have more things in common. This has become the basis of many popular dating and match-making websites: to find a person you have the most in common with.

These four pillars may seem impossible to achieve. How can you find someone to marry who has the same religion, culture, fitness and financial outlook? The purpose of this chapter is not to scare or to discourage you. Rather, it serves as a caution that both of you will have to make adjustments for the differences in your backgrounds. This is difficult to do, but certainly not impossible. The sooner you address these differences, especially before marriage, the greater are your chances of having a harmonious marriage.

- - -

Once, in Pre-Cana (the marriage preparation courses we teach) we met with a couple who had a difference in family cultures and were to be married in a month or two. They spent much of the session arguing with each other over a family tradition of the groom-to-be. His mother desired to have all of her grown children over at her house each Sunday for dinner. This is a beautiful Italian tradition, until… your son is about to marry a girl of another ethnic culture who thinks that that is a bit too much. He thought that his fiancé should make him happy and comply. She thought that he should not demand so much from her. They both thought that it was a case of the future mother-in-law and her future daughter-in-law not liking each other.

What should this couple do? We did not think this was a problem of personality differences, but rather a question of priorities. In marriage, the spouse comes first. The man must not consider his mother's feelings over his fiancé's. Since the couple had conflicting desires, the only solution was a compromise. Maybe they could go for Sunday dinner only once or twice a month with his mother. We should always try to respect the beliefs and traditions of our spouse's families as much as possible, but not at the expense of marital peace.

"There is no perfect marriage, there is no perfect husband, there is no perfect wife... And we will not even mention the mother-in-law!" - Pope Francis

YOU CANNOT CHANGE YOUR SPOUSE AFTER YOU MARRY

There is a saying, "Men marry women hoping they'll never change, but women marry men hoping they will."

What do you do if you are engaged and now realize that you or your fiancé have a missing or very wobbly "pillar"? What will be the consequences? You must sincerely ask yourself: "Can I *really* live with this person for the rest of my life, even if this person doesn't improve?" We are talking about annoying habits, addictions, character defects and the tendency to sin, which we all have to some degree because of Original Sin.

For instance, your fiancé loves to party. You fell in love because they were the life of the party and always in high spirits. Now you realize that they may be an alcoholic. They drink daily; they hide the drinking and they make excuses for their drinking. You must ask yourself, "Can I live with this? Will their excessive drinking lead to abuse? Will it get worse? Will it affect their job, their driving, or any future children?"

How many couples go into marriage thinking that they will change the other person? Some hope their spouse will "magically" change after the wedding vows. Will the spouse really become more mature after you "settle down"? If something needs to change, that person must make an honest effort to change before marriage. Any necessary changes in character traits or habits should happen voluntarily, during the dating or engagement period, out of love for the other.

The fact of the matter is that our "private" decisions affect our spouse, children, grandchildren and community. Take smoking for example, it can lead to serious health consequences, produce second-hand smoke and lead to premature death. We know of a couple where the husband smoked incessantly for decades, and his non-smoking wife died of lung cancer at an early age.

If habits don't change before marriage, they will most likely not change after. In fact, a serious character flaw in a person will probably only get worse, as the pressures of life, marriage and family responsibilities grow.

If there is no resolution during the engagement, you may want to reconsider whether you should get married. Remember: it is better to call off the engagement now than deal with serious consequences later. Seek advice from a parent or a priest, get counseling from a professional.

This does not mean we should seek to marry people without flaws and bad habits. Nobody is perfect! What we want to stress here is that you take a cold, hard look at those flaws before you get married. Then, decide if you could live with that person, warts and all, for the rest of your life.

Once you get married, you should not complain about those things you were aware of before you got married. Now, your job is to live and love the person with those flaws, whether he or she changes or not. No nagging! Remember, after marriage you are "one body"; so respect your spouse as you respect yourself. St. Josemaria Escriva even says that you must love the minor flaws of your spouse, because by patiently dealing with them and silently accepting hardships, you will grow in your spiritual life and achieve heaven.

You can hope that your marriage partner will change their ways. You can pray that your spouse will grow in virtue. You can help that person go to the sacrament of Confession. But the most effective thing you can do is to be the best spouse you can be—understanding, patient and loving. "I urge you to live in a manner worthy of the call... with all humility and gentleness, with patience, bearing with one another through love." Eph. 4:1.

This call to grow in virtue is for every person, at any stage of life. Marriage is particularly challenging at times, and so we should use the years of single life and engagement to prepare ourselves, as we hope our future spouse is doing too.

Sometimes, it is necessary for a couple to break bad habits and go against certain customs of their times. For example, back when we were dating it was common for men and women to greet each other with a kiss on the lips at social events, even if they were mere acquaintances. It was also customary for married people to exchange dance partners which often resulted in flirting, gossip by others, and jealous spouses. We as a couple decided to avoid these customs. We only kissed and danced with each other throughout our courtship and marriage. This is not being prudish—it's being prudent.

DISCUSS THE SPIRITUAL LIFE
AS A COUPLE

"... at every time and in every place, God draws close to man. He calls man to seek him, to know him, to love him with all of his strength."
- Catechism of the Catholic Church 1

At the wedding feast in Cana, Christ changed ordinary water into extraordinarily fine wine. Christ did not change just a few bottles of water, he changed six barrels into wine, so it would fill the wine cellar, and last the newlyweds for years. Engaged couples also hope to change their daily routine into the intoxicating bond of married bliss. But the key is that they can't do this by themselves.

God created us for a relationship with Him. Every one of our hearts was made for eternal and infinite Love, because God is Love. Whether we know it or not, our whole being is oriented toward the divine. But because of sin, we all "fall short of the glory of God." Romans 3:23. Sin separates us from God, from perfect Love. If we continually choose ourselves, our selfishness and serious sin, we risk breaking away completely. We become blind to the spiritual life.

Fortunately for all of us, Jesus is the answer. "For God so loved the world that he gave his only Son, that whoever believes in him should not perish but have eternal life." John 3:16. God respects our free will so instead of forcing us to obey, he invites us to follow Him through Jesus: to get to know Him and befriend Him. Becoming a follower of Jesus means leaving our old self-centered life behind, giving it all over to God and dedicating ourselves to a Christ-centered life. What does that involve?

When we follow Jesus, we get to know His qualities: humility, self-sacrifice, obedience, patience, forgiveness, compassion, and His love. We get to know Him better by reading the Scriptures and by the example of his mother and the saints. We receive his graces through prayer and the Sacraments. If we try to imitate Jesus, we can eventually also hope to acquire some of his virtues—all of which are needed to create a solid marriage and happy family life.

A Christian, especially a Catholic Christian, lives his or her life radically different once they have a true friendship with Christ. For this reason, they should discuss the spiritual life with their significant other, especially if they are contemplating marriage.

Most engaged couples don't quite know where religious beliefs fit into their relationship. They think that their own beliefs should remain a personal secret. They think that it's a private matter, even within the marriage. The men may think religion will inhibit or destroy their sexual life. One or both may be weak in their religious faith. One or the other may be judgmental. They may think religious people are fanatics or unrealistic.

Instead of faith, feelings are now seen as the main marker of a couple's bond. Feelings are not reliable. Talking about feelings is important, but feelings are fickle, ever-changing and often self-centered. They are not enough to carry the responsibility of another human being, and beings, once children arrive. No matter what your feelings are, your values and morals should be part of the conversation you have while dating, and should continue thereafter. If you are a Christian couple, God should be at the core of your relationship and at the center of your homes.

A second grade student raised her hand and told her catechism teacher that God lives in her home. The teacher was amazed: "How do you know?" The little girl replied: "Every morning daddy goes to the bathroom door and shouts: 'God! Are you still in there?'"

Whether it's spending too much time in the bathroom, losing our patience, or any other number of imperfections—sooner or later every couple will realize that they are not perfect, and that they, in fact, do need to improve. That is where Christ comes in. Christianity is all about second, third, fourth and infinite chances to do better.

Your significant other might not be Catholic or Christian, but that does not mean they are not right for you. Go deeper and discuss these important topics—you might be surprised where it will lead you. Here is a great opportunity to share your beliefs and clarify any misunderstandings or doubts about the faith. Just keep in mind, however, that if you both are not of the same faith, you will have to work harder at finding common ground in your marriage.

REALLY GET TO KNOW EACH OTHER

"Not only do men and women communicate differently but they think, feel, perceive, react, respond, love, need, and appreciate differently."
- John Gray, Men Are From Mars, Women Are From Venus

As you can see, there are many important things that a couple needs to coordinate before saying their vows together. They need a clear vision to discern whether their significant other is a solid choice, in all the ways mentioned above. They need to envision and prepare the foundations of their life together. But just when light of love needs to be shed on the relationship more than ever, many turn off the light and jump into bed.

Sex by its very nature is urgent. And so, sex can become a distraction and a priority before truth, trust and temperance have even had a chance to develop. It is undeniable that pre-nuptial sex is a common cause of marriage train-wrecks. The track foundation has not been laid correctly. The tracks are not even, or level, or stable, and the marriage train goes off the rails. Once the train has left the tracks and derailed, the wreckage is a tangle of metal. Disaster! The clean-up is a major task, impacting and wounding many other people. During a nasty divorce, everyone wonders; they were so in love, what happened?

What happened is that the couple might have forgotten where they were headed. As we explained in Section I, the two primary aims of marriage are to foster the love between the spouses, and the procreation of children. Both spouses must be fully engaged to give this gift of themselves and to make the marriage work. The preparations for giving and receiving in marriage require intelligent thought and communication. It involves emotional and spiritual sensitivity.

Dating and engagement is the best time to dream about the future. This is the time when it is especially exciting to find a sweet meeting of minds and hearts, not just a meeting of bodies.

Rushing into physical intimacy is like opening Christmas gifts on Thanksgiving Day. The symbolic meaning and wonder of the gift is lost. Tearing off the wrapping and possessing the gift becomes more important than getting to know the giver and receiving their true love.

Of course, a person can choose to love chastely and begin again. This would mean from the present day onward to abstain from sexual activity till his/her wedding day. And to start seeing sex as a total gift of self, as opposed to a mere physical bonding experience.

If you choose to sacrifice for your beloved in this way, you will be amazed how your relationship will evolve. You'll inevitably learn to express your love in other ways with sweet gestures. Bouquets of flowers, hidden notes, long walks, surprises and serenades—these things will flow from you to your beloved, and later they will serve as a great reminder of how to win over your spouse's affection.

God created Man and Woman separately. Because they were created separately, at different times and for a different purpose, masculinity and femininity differ greatly. It is now fashionable to pretend there is no difference. But there is, and we should celebrate those differences—not try to erase them.

Man was created right after the animals. Perhaps that's why men are hairy, muscular and agile. Woman was the crescendo of God's Creation, created just before His day of rest. Woman was thus meant to be man's beautiful and life-giving companion and to complete what is lacking in the other. Pope Francis stated that a man and a woman need each other to perfect their masculinity and femininity,[7] respectively.

The engagement period is about learning the intricacies of your beloved. As men and women, we often differ in how we like to communicate and receive love. We suggest reading and discussing blogs and books about marriage together. "Men Are From Mars, Women Are From Venus," by John Gray was helpful in understanding how very different men and women are from one another, as though they were from two different planets. If a woman talks about her problems, a man wants to help her to solve them. Whereas, a woman most often only wants to vent and talk about it.

Shortly after our honeymoon, during one of our first arguments, I told my husband, "I just do not understand you!" He replied, "I don't want you to understand me; I want you to love me!" Oddly, it was then that I began to understand him.

Another book we always recommend is "The 5 Love Languages" by Gary Chapman. He writes: "Discovering the primary love language of your spouse is essential if you are to keep his/her emotional love tank full." This addresses the differences in people's temperaments.

The 5 Love Languages Chapman presents are: Words of Affirmation, Quality Time, Receiving Gifts, Acts of Service and Physical Touch. These are five major ways he has observed that people express their love. The key is to learn what is the language of your fiancé or spouse, and to "speak their language," so that they feel loved by you. If you only give him or her the things that you value for yourself, you may make them feel unfulfilled. For instance, take a husband whose "love language" is Acts of Service, and he does many things for his wife, like regularly taking out the garbage or watching the kids. She will certainly appreciate it. However, if her

---

[7] General Audience of Wednesday, 15 April 2015.

love language is Quality Time, she would much prefer and feel deeply loved, if her husband would just spend more time with her.

A person feels the most fulfilled when their spouse gives them what they most desire in a relationship. The lesson here is that we must learn what our spouse truly wants from us, which takes careful observation of the other person's needs and desires. We cannot take them for granted. It takes effective communication by letting your spouse know what it is you really want, instead of expecting the other to always read your mind.

If my husband and I had known this principle when we got married, it would have saved us a lot of guessing and grief. Since my love language is Words of Affirmation, I felt at times that he lacked sensitivity to me, by not wanting to discuss certain things, not noticing my appearance, nor commenting on a special meal I prepared.

His love language is Physical Touch. At times he did not feel loved, because I spent more time talking to him rather than touching. I would ask him: "How was your day?" which he knew was considerate of me, but he wanted to forget about his stressful day. He would have much preferred a simple neck rub or hand massage to show my concern or love.

Over the years, we always knew that we loved each other very much, yet at times it felt like something was missing. It was often these little—yet not so little—acts of love in the correct "love language" that were lacking. Even now, after so many years of marriage, we have to remind each other of our love language. *"Honey, what do you think of this lovely dinner I prepared...?"*

COHABITATION

"Marriage is more than a fleeting fashion; it is of enduring importance. Its essence derives from our human nature and social character." - Pope Francis, Amoris Laetitia (The Joy of Love)

Most of the couples that we meet with in Catholic Marriage Prep (Pre-Cana) are already living together, at least 90 percent. Why are so many couples cohabitating today, even though there is a higher risk for divorce?

There are many reasons why couples choose to cohabitate. Whether it be a fear of total commitment, an attempt to avoid divorce, a need for economic security or a way to test out the relationship—the reasoning seems viable and responsible.

For many women cohabitation is seen as a step towards the commitment they really want. For men, it is often a means of escaping that commitment while getting the benefits of a marriage. Sometimes those roles are reversed. Either way, there is a loss of understanding and intentionality. It's like "playing house" or conducting an experiment. Unfortunately, the couple's experiment in compatibility actually damages the budding relationship. Cohabitation by its very nature is conditional and temporary. It cannot test something that is meant to be permanent.

Cohabitation is essentially an internal disposition: "We will stay with one another until you, or I, find something or someone better."

Pope Francis wrote an apostolic exhortation, "Amoris Laetitia, The Joy of Love," which we've referred to many times throughout the book. He analyzes the present "throw-away secular culture" as it impacts marriage. "Committing oneself exclusively and definitively to another person always involves a risk and a bold gamble.

Unwillingness to make such a commitment is selfish, calculating and petty. It fails to recognize the rights of another person and to present him or her to society as someone worthy of unconditional love."

When we ask couples we mentor who are living together, or in a civil marriage, why they finally decided to get married in the church, they can't quite answer this question. The woman usually says: "It was time." The man typically shrugs and goes along with the woman's decision.

A groom surprised his bride by bringing golf clubs to their wedding.
The bride asked: "Honey, why did you bring the golf clubs?"
"Is this going to take all day?" he replied.

We're always thrilled when a couple decides to do a church wedding. However, it would be much better if they understood why they need God, what is grace, and why sacramental marriage is permanent and the real deal. Civil weddings and common law marriage of a man and a woman existed in every culture before Christ, as did divorce. Jesus Christ brought it to a new level—the Divine level. As Christians we believe that sacramental grace gives us unique and essential spiritual assistance throughout the marriage and a consistent focus on the Divine Plan.

If you are cohabitating, as many young couples are, there is a chance to set things right. Once you've discussed your beliefs, talk about what that means for your relationship and living situation. If you are a couple wanting to live out a Christian relationship—you can begin again, whenever you so choose. Even if the marriage is a week away, embrace chastity now, and wait to embrace your spouse in bed until after the marriage vows. This will set you on a new and beautiful path to appreciating each other, and your marriage, in a new light.

PRE-CANA CLASSES

"Marriage is like building a house. 'You would not wish to build it on the shifting sands of emotions, but on the rock of true love, the love that comes from God.'" - Pope Francis, Address to Engaged Couples

In the hippie days, the mantra for better relationships was "free love," "let go," "chill out!" After a few decades, psychologists acknowledged that this approach was not working. This was evident in couples therapy where things often stayed superficial or stifled. Whether it was a lack of respect for the spouse, a wound that festered, a refusal to forgive or a desire for revenge—what it came down to was often selfish desire.

The next generation of psychologists tried to go deeper into the human psyche. They wanted to help the estranged couple rekindle their earlier friendship, to reminisce about what brought them together, to identify and reject what drove them apart, to examine what irked them, to acknowledge one's own shortcomings and to learn to forgive. This is certainly a step in the right direction, but with the present staggering divorce rates, it clearly is not enough.

The newest Catholic psychology of marriage is still being fully developed. It adds a theological element. Based on the New Testament, it highlights the great dignity of each person, as a unique child of God. It teaches the importance of marriage life as a reflection of the Love of God for each person. It appeals to the special graces inherent in the Sacrament of Matrimony. Not only does it urge couples to humility and forgiveness, but it also gives us concrete ways to achieve them. It presents a model, that of the Holy Family: Jesus, Mary and Joseph. In short, it promotes a marriage based on what God has in mind for each of us.

Pre-Cana is preparation for couples who want to learn more and prepare for a marriage based on the Catholic faith. A parish priest in Chicago invited us to teach Pre-Cana classes because of our enthusiasm in living our faith and our willingness to share our thoughts. At the time, we were married about 30 years and were raising eight children from college age to grammar school.

Rima also successfully taught confirmation class and religious education to teenagers for 20 years! Her home experience with children of all ages was the best training for that challenging work.

These days it is so easy to be a "Christian," have a pagan philosophy, and live like an atheist. In other words, just do what everyone else is doing. That means: have fun, get the most out of life and look out for "number one." To be young means to have a good time, enjoy the opposite sex, explore your sexual attractions and later "settle down" when your friends pair off and the party days seem to be over...

Daughter: "Mommy, why is the bride wearing such a nice white dress?
Mother: "This is the happiest day of her life. She's getting married today!
She wants to show her happiness to her family and to everyone here."
"Oh," said the child, "Mommy, why is the young man wearing black?"

All jokes aside, the statistics that engaged couples face these days are no laughing matter. There is a 50% probability that any couple will divorce within seven years. (If you cohabitate before marriage, 75% will divorce, according to the book, *Marriage Insurance.*[8]) Of those 50% who do not divorce, only 10% of those who stay together say they have a happy marriage. The remaining 40% just tolerate their marital situation. So, overall, only a fraction of all couples who

---

[8] JCD Rev. Francis J. Hoffman, *Marriage Insurance: 12 Rules To Live By* (Relevant Radio; First Edition: 2013).

marry make it to the "happy" stage of a lifetime marriage. No wonder the young generation hesitates to "tie the knot!"

The stats are clearly working against us. What can you do to prepare against these odds? Engaged couples should get serious and realize that they can no longer mix the teachings of Christianity with soft-core hedonism and hard-core materialism. This is spiritual schizophrenia.

Sooner rather than later, a split personality will split up the marriage. The lack of Christian virtues within the marriage results in lesser respect of the spouse, verbal and physical abuse, possibly infidelity, the acrimonious divorce process itself, and scars in the memory and psyche. PMSD, post-marriage stress disorder, is a very real and under-diagnosed syndrome. The best treatment is prevention, and, of course, communication and forgiveness.

In our Pre-Cana encounters with couples of many backgrounds, we offer them a Christian vision of marriage. This includes the "Universal Call to Holiness," lived out by early Christians and the ground-breaking "Theology of the Body," presented by Saint Pope John Paul II. These are great concepts but they are not easily understood.

We came up with the term "Nuptial Spirituality" as a way to define and combine these fundamental ideas. People these days like the idea of being spiritual, but may not have thought that they can live out their spirituality together as a married couple. Nuptial Spirituality is a framework for seeking holiness together and living out a total giving of self to one's spouse.

When we marry, our path on Earth is with our spouse. Our path to Heaven should not be seen as just a personal journey. We always travel with our spouse, hand in hand.

- - -

As a practicing physician, Linas is trained to focus on human pathology, on the etiology of pain and suffering, and what is going wrong or will go wrong. He focuses on the negatives and the necessary therapies.

Rima, a philosophy major and artistic soul, focuses on the positive aspects of marriage, on beauty, and what should be done to live a joyful life together. This allows us to give a balanced perspective to our Pre-Cana couples, and hopefully now to all our readers.

SECTION III

ONCE YOU'VE SAID "I DO"

Our wedding was everything I could have dreamed it to be. It was a big, beautiful Lithuanian wedding with all the trappings and traditions. Both sides of the family were very happy for this match. We could not wait to start our new life together and to prove our love for each other. For us, that meant we were ready to give of ourselves completely and to be open to life.

The first big challenge was that immediately after our honeymoon, Linas had to balance his Ophthalmology residency at the University of Chicago with intense preparation for his board exams which would be held within a year. Our future depended on the results.

Our next challenge was that after two months of wedded bliss, we were already expecting our first child. I managed to get through most of my nauseous pregnancy while working downtown in a law firm, and Linas passed his boards on his first try. Most importantly, we managed to make time for each other and to keep happy.

After two years of living in the Lithuanian neighborhood in Southside Chicago where I grew up, we moved to Gainesville, Florida with our one-year old daughter, because Linas accepted a Fellowship at the University of Florida to do corneal transplants.

We loved Florida, because it was like a yearlong honeymoon. We were in an entirely different place, with new friends, an easier pace, and warmer climate. We lived in a townhouse complex with two swimming pools on one side, and a picturesque swamp with alligators and herons on the other. Since we had no family or community nearby, we had to depend solely on one another, and God, for moral support.

COMING TOGETHER AS ONE

"And the two will become one flesh. So they are no longer two, but one flesh." - Mark 10:8

Once you've said "I do" your relationship takes on a whole new meaning. This is what the wedding celebration is all about! You are now one with your beloved. Your mind, body and soul comes together with the other. Even on a biological level, your bodies are releasing powerful hormones in the brain such as oxytocin and vasopressin which are meant to bond you to one another.

In the marital act, you are in a very real sense re-expressing your marriage vows through your bodies. It is probably the most authentic sign of the deep, personal allegiance you made to each other. The vows you made at your wedding ceremony are reaffirmed: you come together freely, wholeheartedly; you're prepared to accept children and to love and honor each other.

For most couples, and especially those who lived out a chaste courtship, these first few months are life-changing and heavenly. As they should be! A honeymoon and a joined life together is full of brimming hope and excitement.

That doesn't mean there won't be early arguments and difficulties. Imagine the impossible you are trying to attain: two grown adults who have distinctly different genders, personalities, habits and needs are coming together as one. You feel unified when things are going well, but pulled far apart when things are rough. That is inevitable with our sinful, fallen nature. However, if both of you believe in the permanence in marriage, you will be able to trust that the other person will do what it takes to solve problems or resolve differences. You will not give up because things get tough.

In your dating and engagement period, and especially in your early married life, be sure to create a respectful dynamic between the two of you. The patterns you put in place now could set the tone for your entire marriage. It is very important to respect your spouse deeply, because by living so intimately with one another, you are bound to see each others faults more clearly. You are bound to be disappointed in some areas of your shared life within the first year. You may even be disillusioned with your spouse or marriage itself.

However, this moving out of the emotional high and into your commitment to each other, is when real love begins. Your love is tested—sometimes by fire or even by ice. In these times, you must choose the good of the other and be willing to sacrifice your feelings, opinions or preferences at least for a time.

There have been various times in our marriage when our relationship was stressed and strained. However, by really being "committed" to one another, we always found our way back to peace and joy. One time, the cause for strain was something which at first seemed like an emotional problem, but the cause turned out to be physical. I (Rima) was feeling so burnt out, that I lost enthusiasm or desire for anything. I attributed this to the strain of raising the kids. I was not feeling very affectionate with my husband, and he thought I was neglecting him. It turned out that I was severely anemic. This condition was resolved after three months of iron supplements and the loving support of my husband. Our relationship once again became not only normal, but better than ever.

There are even some problems, personal or physical, which can never seem to be resolved, yet we learn to live with them, together. In the bigger picture, these problems are ultimately accepted as minor. As long as you know that the other will never leave you, no matter what the challenge, you can learn to accept every difficulty...

MATURITY IN MARRIAGE

A young man came to ask a father for his daughter's hand in marriage.
Before answering, the father asked a few questions:
Father: "You live in an apartment with three other guys. Where will you
live if you get married?"
Young man: "I don't yet know, but I have Faith—God will provide."
Father: "You don't have a degree or a stable job. How will you support my
daughter as your wife?"
Young man: "There are a few issues to face, but I'm deeply in love with your
daughter. I know God helps those who trust in Him—God will provide!"
The young man left, and the excited mother rushed into the room.
Mother: "So... how'd it go?"
Father: "He's a nice young man. But there's just one problem... He thinks
I'm God."

There are three basic stages in life: infancy, adolescence and adulthood. The first stage, infancy, is total dependence. The baby is breastfed, the diaper changed regularly. The cute baby is the center of attention and can do no wrong. The world revolves around him or her.

The next stage is adolescence, or teen years: a state of reckless behavior and crazy rebellion. Teenagers are usually best behaved when they want something: to drive the car, to stay out late or to be liked by their peers. Because of their change in hormones they are frequently sullen, cynical and withdrawn.

The adult state is a time of independence: a steady job, marriage and family responsibilities. The mature adult is someone who cares for others and is not totally absorbed in their own things. They participate in community, cultural and religious activities because they are social and have a sense of duty. Deep down a mature man wants to leave the bachelor life behind and build a solid family legacy. The mature woman wants to exchange dating apps for a good husband and a wonderful family.

A person should mature through these three stages of life, and they must do it in time and on time. Otherwise, there can be serious problems in the future. It may seem like maturity is inevitable as we grow older. But unfortunately age and maturity do not always grow simultaneously. Many people never fully mature. Someone who is selfish in their thinking and in their actions will always be childish. His/her own needs and wants are really their first priority. This will lead the other spouse to feel exhausted and alone.

Hopefully, a mature woman finds and marries a sufficiently mature man and vice versa. They have to show real signs of maturity before marriage, however, we all have room for growth. Both the husband and wife should learn true maturity through marriage and parenthood. This is because the hallmark of maturity is thinking about, and taking care of others.

Maturity is being responsible to others. Pope John Paul II emphasizes this in "Love and Responsibility": "The capacity to love is determined by the fact that man is ready to seek the good consciously with others, to subordinate himself to this good because of others, or to subordinate himself to others because of this good." In other words, the more responsibility you feel for others—namely, your spouse and children—the greater your capacity to love them.

In marriage, this means praying for and with each other and giving up your own comforts for their sake. It means going to work cheerfully to help the family, coming home to dinner, making dinnertime special, spending quality time with each other and expressing love the way your spouse most desires. These habits should be formed early on in the marriage so that they continue when life gets busier.

A DECISION OF THE WILL,
NOT THE EMOTIONS

How many psychologists does it take to change a light bulb?
One, but the light bulb must really want to change!

When a couple marries, they expect and hope the light of love will shine forever. The energy of sexual attraction and the excitement of a new situation, may keep the light burning for a while, but then they realize that something is lacking. There is no unity. They don't want to change or compromise, they want their new spouse to change or admit they are wrong.

As noted in the previous chapter, the couple might come to realize that they are not "sufficiently mature," and they start to argue and fight frequently. At this point the marriage will either suffer or strengthen. When conflict first appears after marriage, the couple should "assume an active and creative role," grow in maturity, develop empathy, and do whatever it takes to make the marriage work. Sometimes a marriage counselor is necessary.

The first thing to notice is that to keep loving your spouse in marriage is a decision of the will, not the emotions. The couple does not necessarily "feel" like changing, they make a conscious decision to change. Like the light bulb, they need to want to change!

They would do well to remember that the priest during their wedding ceremony did not ask whether they "loved" one another, he asked them if they "take" the other for their spouse. Thus the emphasis is on their decision rather their feelings. The phrase: "I do" is a personal, rational statement and a public commitment, not an emotional response. This is a sacred covenant, not a time-limited contract. It's done in a sacred space, because the immutable God is a witness to your permanent commitment.

Because our culture has become self-obsessed and self-absorbed, everyone is conditioned to be very individualistic. We think primarily about ourselves. We all want to know: What's in it for me? Is the other person really trying to please me? We are unprepared for an exclusive, unselfish commitment to the other in a permanent marriage relationship. Our culture exalts the individual, not the family, as the basic unit of society. The family exists for *me* and *my needs*, and so I will opt out whenever I fall out of "love." It's "my body" and I will take it wherever I want to.

When a person is truly ready to marry, they make an interior decision of the will. "I will love you no matter what you do or say, or what you fail to do or say. I am committed to this relationship no matter what!" This is unconditional giving: the complete gift of self. It is said out loud, publicly, in the wedding vows. It is then also expressed in the sexual act. The body is no longer mine, but ours, made to be together.

The union of two filaments of a light bulb emit radiant energy. If the two filaments separate, the bulb is cold. It is useless. Two people in a marriage together emit spiritual energy, a product of their love. It gives light to those around them. The world becomes brighter, happier and full of color.

When two people fall in love, they may think it is their own personal matter. But when they get married, they form a society. Parents, siblings, relatives, friends, community and church are also involved in their family, the basic unit of society. Everyone is excited and expecting great things from them. They are also expecting to see children—the new generation. The parents are so happy to become grandparents!

At a wedding, the couple and the community are full of joy and hope. However, the couple needs more than just human hope, celebrations, "wishful thinking," and the feeling that their love will last forever. By placing their expectations of lasting happiness solely in another human being, spouses will inevitably be disillusioned and disappointed. It is God who is the source of all Love. He is the invisible electric current which gives the two filaments the capacity to give light. He is the Light of the World. God makes all things new and exciting!

In marriage, the couple begin a spiritual journey to live for each other, for their children, for others. They mature in love and "become more of a man and more of a woman in the process," as Pope Francis writes in "Amoris Laetitia." This will not always be an easy process.

- *A patient was being discharged from the intensive care unit and the doctor asked to talk to the patient's spouse.*
- *The doctor told the spouse that the patient was still in a very fragile state, and that continuous, meticulous home care was needed.*
- *It was also very important not to upset the patient's emotions nor to criticize. The spouse should humor and cater to every whim, like breakfast in bed, massages and giving them the TV control.*
- *As they drove home, the patient asked the spouse what the doctor said.*
- *"He said he doesn't think you'll live very long."*

OPEN TO LIFE

"To have a large family, if such is the will of God, is a guarantee of happiness and effectiveness, in spite of everything that the mistaken proponents of a life based on selfish pleasure may say." - St. Josemaria Escriva, "Christ Is Passing By"

Being open to life is not always easy. The Catholic comedian, Jim Gaffigan, put it this way—he said having a fifth child feels like you're neck deep, drowning—and someone throws you a baby! He also said he loves his kids dearly, but when the last one was born, he called the children together and told them: "I love you all, but now one of you has to go..." And when people ask him if he plans to have any more kids, he answers that he doesn't know, and calls out to his wife: "Hey Honey, are you expecting?"

People think Catholics are irresponsible for having big families, that we have no self-control, or that we have lots of kids just because the Church tells us to. But that is not what the Catholic Church teaches. What they do teach is that in chaste sexual union, a married couple mirrors God's unselfish love and His creative power. Thus, sex has a dual purpose. One that is *unitive* (bonding the couple in love) and *procreative* (welcoming new life). When one of these two purposes is absent, sex becomes a selfish act. Chastity in marriage is this complete gift of the self exclusively to one's spouse and being open to life in the sexual act.

Catholics welcome children because they are a visible sign of our love of our spouse, and our love of God. We are awed by this power to be co-creators of life. We marvel at the trust God has in us by giving us each child. Each child is a treasure. We are called to serve, and there is no lack of opportunity to serve in a large family.

Everyone learns generosity and a spirit of service. Each child adds a burden; but also multiplies the joys. The multiple joys far outweigh the difficulties.

These days pregnancy is feared like never before, but paradoxically, being "open to life" can be very liberating.

The question is this: will you give yourself, and your body, to be used by the Divine Creator to bring new life into this world, or will you give in to the prevalent culture that says you are in control, the sole master of your body?

Currently there is a big push to place one's personal dreams and ambitions or social issues above family. We believe family and babies are part of the equation—they make dreams more fruitful, beautiful and always interesting. We can testify that there is never a dull moment in a large family!

Material wealth, beauty, prestige—those are all good things, but trivial and temporal when compared to eternal souls being brought into existence. You are cooperating with God and your spouse to accomplish this. We should all be very humbled by this creative power. Resolve not to undermine it by creating obstacles instead of creating life. God's first commandment to Adam and Eve was, "Be fruitful and multiply!" (Gn 1:28).

You said "I do," now "Do it!" At a Catholic ceremony, the couple is asked by the priest: "Are you willing to accept children from God?" So, don't postpone children until such-and-such a financial goal is met, as many seem to do these days. Welcome children on God's timetable, not yours. We would argue that if a couple cannot support a child nine months after their wedding, be it financially, physically or mentally, they probably are not ready for marriage. However, if they absolutely want to get married at that time, the Church allows them to postpone children in a non-contraceptive way, which is not the easiest way to start a marriage.

It is not Catholic teaching, however, to have as many children as biologically possible throughout the fertile years of married life. Life imposes limits. Modern life brings more stress, especially when both spouses need to work full-time, making it very challenging to raise children. Every couple's situation is different, just as every social era has its own particular challenges.

There are limits on responsible procreation: physical, emotional health, financial… However, to space out births, a Catholic couple must never use contraception, but rather, Natural Family Planning, after consulting with their spiritual director. NFP is usually introduced or taught in Marriage Preparation courses.

Natural Family Planning, NFP, is the natural way to defer pregnancy by adjusting sexual activity to infertile periods. No contraceptives or barriers are used or needed, and there are no dangerous chemicals ingested or coils implanted in the uterus. More importantly, NFP is not "Catholic birth control" because new life is not blocked or prevented. Rather, the couple relies on "self-control," abstaining from intercourse for a time.

NFP does require a serious reason. Its purpose is to space out births. The couple should inform their conscience about this very personal issue and also consult with their priest. If the couple decides NFP is necessary to space out births, close communication is needed between the spouses during those periods of abstinence during the fertile period. Many couples will find NFP very difficult and even frustrating at times.

Abstinence is the practice of restraining oneself from enjoying something that gives pleasure. This concept of delayed gratification in food, drink and sex, may be something new to one or both spouses, so it takes getting used to. Perhaps some people are frustrated or lose patience with NFP, because it is like dieting. Dieting can be a good thing for our health, but it is not meant to be a way of life. It is meant to be used for only limited periods of time.

Training the will to restrain oneself takes courage and self-control. However, NFP is so important that it will take more than self-control. To be really successful with NFP, the couple needs to rely on supernatural means: prayer and the frequent use of the sacraments.

Some couples say that using Natural Family Planning rather than artificial birth control can enhance a spouse's intimacy and sexual satisfaction. The periods of abstinence in couples who practice NFP within a spiritual framework can create a renewed sense of longing for one another. That longing can bring them back together again with even more passion than before. This is referred to by NFP couples as the "honeymoon effect." Although many NFP couples say that this is not their experience, practicing NFP can at the very least contribute to making their marriage stronger, to "marriage-building." No matter what their experience is of practicing NFP, we believe God will bless couples for their efforts in trying to exercise "responsible parenthood" rather than resorting to contraception.

Christopher West writes in his book, "Good News About Sex and Marriage,": "Every married couple is called to be 'fruitful and multiply' (Gn 1:28). This is the starting point. Children are not something tacked on to married love but are the crowning glory of married love. Thus, instead of avoiding children, the general disposition should be the receiving of children as they come, unless a couple has a good reason not to."

We did not use NFP in our marriage. We were always open to having "as many children as God wanted us to have." This of course is not possible for everyone, but we started marriage firmly supported on all "four pillars." We felt that we were able to be generous with God. "Everyone to whom much is given, much is required" (Luke 12:48). This attitude was both challenging, yet liberating. It was exciting for us to continue the work of "Creation" and to see what God had in store for us. He rewarded us with great joy and eight marvelous children!

SECTION IV
PARENTHOOD

Parenthood is a big adjustment for any couple. We were no exception. Nothing can prepare you for the sleepless nights, the aching body and the responsibility of keeping another being alive! Linas and I were a real team. He was very hands-on as a dad, which was rare in those days. There were many nights where he would get up to change diapers and walk a fussy baby around for an hour or two, even though he would have to start work early in the morning.

In our family, the most difficult combination was having two, five and eight kids. Two because they were still very young and needy. It was a tug-of-war for attention. I'd be nursing the baby, and the toddler would be climbing all over me. When expecting the third, I cried often to myself thinking it would be too much. However, God helped us and gradually the other kids became an asset: providing help to me and entertaining each other. Three was actually easier to handle than two!

Five became difficult again because they were all still very young children and could help only so much. Four were still in diapers at night. Up to this point I could handle the kids and the house by myself, with support from Linas. He would run errands, buy groceries and often take the kids for outings. However, with five kids, we needed outside help: a regular babysitter 2-3 times a week and a house cleaner twice a month. They were a great, and very necessary addition to family management.

This was great until eight kids, when the disparate demands of schools and after-school activities "drove me crazy." At one point we had children in five different schools: pre-school, grammar school, junior high, high school and college, all of which pulled us in very different directions. It was a never-ending cycle for years.

Then the oldest children got driver's licenses and could take the younger kids to activities. Important help, just in time! Maintaining the routine of regular dinner time, chauffeuring children, limiting sports and video-gaming, persevering with our family hour and family Rosary became even more important. Linas and I also tried our best to keep regular private date nights, which included a very much needed glass of red wine.

THE MIRACLE OF NEW LIFE

"You wove me in my mother's womb. I will give thanks to You, for I am fearfully and wonderfully made. Wonderful are your works." - Psalm 139:14

The arrival of the first child is truly a blessed miracle. The physical presence of a newborn baby is amazing! Here is a marvelous new creation. It defies understanding. It makes us so happy! It brings us into close contact with the Creator.

Rima says that she could detect the dominant personality traits of our kids in the first 24 hours after birth. I as the father could only see that the baby is sleeping or awake, the eyes are open or closed. The mother sees much more. She discovers each child's temperaments while the newborn is feeding and interacting with her: curious, calm, sweet, energetic, funny, independent, persistent, or demanding.

The father may be the "head-of-the-family," but the mother is certainly the heart. The mother sees with her eyes and heart what is going on with the family. The father often gets his daily "briefing" from the wife. If the father is smart, he will avoid "heartache" in the family by not stressing out his spouse. "Husbands, love your wives, and do not be harsh with them," Col. 3:19. Remember the saying: "Happy wife, happy life."

A newborn is totally helpless. It is totally dependent on the parents to be fed, to stay warm, to be cleaned. New mothers instinctively rises to the occasion. The young lady becomes a mother, and she stays a mother all of her life. Her center of gravity has again shifted from herself, to her spouse, and now to her newborn. Her most eager desire is to give of herself: her love, her attention, even physically, her milk.

As great as that sounds, motherhood is far from glamorous. Babies spit up and vomit on her shoulder. They cry, stink and poop often. When it's time to wash the baby, it can be like wrestling a greased piglet. Changing baby boys may result in urine in the face. When they're old enough to roll away, they must be quickly caught by the leg before they fall off the bed. Babies cry. Often and loud. The mother is seriously sleep-deprived, but must continue to work inside and/or out of the home, even if sick. She is giving away so much of herself to her child. She is always the center. Like the solar system, the children tend to revolve around her.

This is where fathers need to make an extra effort, like a gallant knight in shining armor. When we were growing up, our fathers kept their distance, they were not "hands on." Fathers need to rescue their beloved wives from the constant demands of motherhood. Women need extra tenderness and support in this demanding time. Men should pitch in and help with all chores. The father must ease the burdens of the new mother, like cooking suppers and taking some or all of the children out of the house for a few hours to give her a break. Be as engaged as possible at home, even when tired and sleep-deprived. Take time to appreciate your newborn, even if you have a hard time connecting to the infant at first.

That cuddly little human will develop new powers amazingly quickly. They will become aware of time, and the passage of time. That child will start thinking about the future and what the future will bring. They will discover the power to imagine, and imagine various possibilities: even monsters in the closet or under the bed. A child will wonder and ask questions, many questions. Get ready to answer lots of them. Kids are typically very interested in the "big" questions, about death, eternity, angels, God. Their physical and mental development is incredible, their logic can be comical and at times profound. Their spiritual capacity is truly amazing.

We would often talk to our children about these things. Remembering angels at bedtime, for instance, would help the kids go to sleep and prevent nightmares. The stories of saints would capture their imagination, and the fact that they could pray to them made it even more fascinating. Of course, we always made sure that they knew that God loves them, and that we love Him and each other, too.

Our nine-year-old daughter once said that whenever she thought about God "who always was and always will be," her head would start spinning, and she needed to lie down.

One morning while enjoying a family breakfast, our five-year-old daughter stood up with a big smile on her face and announced: "I can't wait to die!" We all fell silent and waited for her to finish. "...because in heaven we won't have to eat scrambled eggs anymore!"

Now our grandchildren entertain us with their anecdotes. They call Jesus, "Baby Amen!", "The King of the Jewels!" (instead of King of the Jews).

Our four-year-old grandson shouts, "I love church! Church is my favorite." When there was a short service at Ash Wednesday, he complained, "Hey! I didn't have enough time to pray for all of my cousins." He had fourteen cousins, after all.

Our four-year old granddaughter was praying out loud to God at bedtime, saying she was sorry that she gave her grandmother her cold. When her mother tried to interject, saying it wasn't her fault, her daughter replied: "Excuse me, Mama, but I am talking to God!"

As parents and grandparents, it's up to us to instill this sense of wonder in children, an awareness of God's presence in their lives, and they will take it from there. They will fill you with wonder and delight a hundredfold. Moreover, they will grow up to be men and women of character and faith.

PRIORITIES IN FAMILY LIFE

"Let your children see that God is not only on your lips, but also in your deeds; that you are trying to be loyal and sincere, and that you love each other and you really love them too." - St. Josemaria Escriva, "Christ is Passing By"

Once you have established what your shared values are as a couple in marriage, such as are found in the four pillars of marriage: Faith, Family, Fitness, Finances, it is very important to have a clear agreement on priorities. We have tried to live by these:

God comes first above all.
Spouse before children.
Children before self.
Family before all others.

Everyone can see that God, spouse, children and family are very important, but it can be difficult to see why in that order. We know many people who share these same values, but have switched up the priorities. Mothers, for example, have a tendency to put their children, and their activities, first. In time this can negatively affect the marriage.

First Priority is God. God comes first, or at least He should come first, but in daily life, "our hearts are far from Him." Isaiah 29:13. There needs to be a plan for your prayer life otherwise it can easily slip. Prayer is the way to communicate with God, to get closer to Him, and through Him, learn to love better.

As practicing Catholics there are many ways to stay in the presence of God throughout the day. You can wake up and say the Morning Offering. Spiritual Reading or Mental Prayer are ways to converse with God. Daily Mass is available each day of the work week in many parishes. The Rosary is a contemplative prayer that we say as a couple or with the children every now and then, usually in the evenings.

In our family, Linas would lead the Rosary, start prayer before meals, drive the family to Sunday Mass or to Saturday Confession. It is also very important to explain what it is *all* about. We noticed that the kids pay more attention, and seem to give it more weight when the father takes the lead. "When a strong man, fully armed, guards his own house, his possessions are safe." Luke 11:21. The husband should be that "strong man." Many fathers may have religious faith, but have not thought about taking responsibility for the spiritual tone of their house, relegating that role to the mother. When a father and mother answer to a "higher authority," then the children will truly learn to revere their parents, and ultimately to love and serve their Father, God.

Second Priority is your Spouse. We raised a family of eight children. You can imagine how much time and energy that took. However, we always made time for each other as a couple. Note, I did not say "we found time for each other." With children, you will never "find time" and even less so, will you find the extra energy. We had to "make time" for each other each day.

During the day, I was totally dedicated to the kids, but when their father would come home, the focus was on him. We welcomed him home with great joy. Everything was already prepared for dinner time, followed by family hour with both parents, bedtime preparation for the kids, then alone time for the parents. This takes planning!

Our daughter, who has four little children, has worked full-time throughout most of her marriage and makes time to be alone with her husband each evening. They mastered getting their kids to bed on time. The philosophy is that the children revolve around the parents—not the parents around the children. It is very good for children to know that they are not the center of the universe.

The Third Priority is Children. Children before self is the third priority. Of course, we place our children's needs before our own needs and household duties. However, mothers tend to place their children first even before their spouse. Unless she orders her day carefully, there will be no time or energy for God or spouse. Loving parents mistakenly allow their kids to walk all over them if they do not set limits, like a strict bedtime schedule. Otherwise little kids will be found wandering the halls and demanding attention all night. Teenagers will be playing video games, watching TV and then asking you for help with their homework during your bedtime.

On the other hand, there are parents who lose their focus on the children and give too much time and attention to their careers, parents, siblings, friends, TV, media, fitness and hobbies. They relegate the upbringing of their children to nannies, teachers, and coaches. Then, their kids may end up with values totally different from their own.

As parents, you must find the balance between how much of your own time and attention you give to your children, and how much you depend on others to form your children. There is no greater gift you can give your children, nor greater lesson than the faithful love between the spouses. If the parents keep God and Spouse their two top priorities, they are already half way to raising their children well!

The Fourth Priority is Family: Family comes before the outside: work, school, activities, relatives, friends. With busy schedules, dinner is one way to ensure family stays a top priority. Dinner was so vital, even sacred, for stable family life, that for many years we did not allow sports or other activities to interfere with dinnertime. At the dinner table, we would always begin with a prayer. While I was busy serving the meal, my husband would start the dinner conversation—something interesting and informative. It is at the dinner table that children learned their manners and how to converse intelligently. Years ago, we heard of a study that reported that children who ate dinner regularly with both parents had higher IQ's. We never watched TV during dinner, and only on rare occasions after dinner. This gave us lots of time to spend with each other. Let your kids, not the TV, entertain you and one another.

After dinner, we almost always had what was to become a hallmark Sidrys Family Tradition: *"Family Hour."* Both of us parents and all the children would spend up to an hour just *being* with each other. Yes, without any plan, we would simply relax and enjoy each other's company. We would just sit around the family room and talk about everyone's day, tell jokes, share family history, talk politics, plan trips. The kids would horse around, put on shows, sing, dance, recite poetry, play games, practice foreign languages, roller-skate, play ping pong or foosball in the basement, etc... We loved just being together. Afterwards, we spent another hour putting all the younger ones to bed: brushing teeth, baths, reading stories, singing, and night prayers.

Our children say that to this day, what they remember most fondly about us and what defines us as a family, was the tradition of our "Family Hour." Try to form traditions in your own family which will bond you to each other.

REST REQUIRED

"Leisure is only possible when we are at one with ourselves. We tend to overwork as a means of self-escape, as a way of trying to justify our existence." - Josef Pieper, "Leisure: The Basis of Culture"

Life can quickly become overwhelming and so, to keep your sanity, you need to rest. Rest is defined as either sleep, or freedom from your routine work, or a state of motionlessness. Rest can also be a state of spiritual peace and tranquility. This is the type of rest that we really need!

The philosophy book, "Leisure, the Basis of Culture" notes that rest and silence is the basis of a contemplative spirit. This leisure, a form of inner silence, is intimately connected to the worship of God. There is no true rest if there is no connection to the Divine.

This may seem difficult to understand. However, in the story of creation, we are told that God rested on the seventh day. Did God really need to rest on the seventh day? No, the moral of this story is for our benefit. It is the devil that does not rest, but constantly prowls around, looking for the ruin of souls (Peter 5:8).

This commandment to rest is difficult for Americans to accept. The capitalist culture we live in now is built on work. We want to succeed. We want our share of the pie. What were considered to be luxuries have now become necessities. Americans work the longest hours and take the shortest vacations. This affects our health and well-being. It destroys marriages.

Even grade school children are no longer allowed free time to play, rest and just be kids. They are over-scheduled with activities. The sports teams have become ultra competitive, the coaches very demanding, and the practices more and more numerous. Games and practice times are now scheduled for Sunday mornings, crowding out critical family time and religious worship.

We must learn to say: "No! Enough is enough." We place limits on activity and give priority to our own physical, mental and spiritual health. We do not want to endanger our marriages with neglect or fatigue. We do not want to see our kids suffer burnout by seventh grade. We do not want our family members reaching for drugs or alcohol to alleviate sports injuries, emotional stress and lack of rest.

Let us return to the basics. Start by resting on Sundays. Your duty to the Lord's day is to worship God and to thank Him. This also involves enjoying your family and your life by placing God at the center of your life. "Be still and know that I am your God." Psalm 46:10. Of all our family devotions, Mass was a non-negotiable. As long as our children lived in our house, we all went to Mass together on Sundays and holy days. No questions asked.

We do not go to Mass because we *feel* like it, but because God *wills* it. We go to Mass to show God our deep gratitude for all the blessings that He has given us. All of our children have gone to Mass all of their lives, including their college days, and now with their own families.

Most Catholics view this Commandment to keep holy the Lord's day as merely a requirement to go to church. However, that hour in church is not all God wants from us. God wants us to keep holy the entire day. We must rest on the Lord's Day, just like God rested on the seventh day. It is no wonder that the Hebrews and Jews throughout history have a highly developed sense of culture, because they took the Sabbath so seriously, not even cooking on that day. It is a day meant not for work, but for enjoyment of the fruits of one's labor.

The business world frequently requires employees to come in early and to stay late, just to demonstrate their loyalty to their boss or company. The cell phone keeps ringing with questions, news and assignments even when at home and on Sundays. Over time, this can be quite dangerous to your health. Burnout is mentally debilitating and physically crippling, affecting both your job and family.

How does one rest when one has little children running around, and unfinished work to do? Do only what is absolutely necessary. Ask others to pitch in and help with the kids. Do not feel obligated to do yard-work or finish other projects. Do not worry. We truly rest by developing the correct attitude. You are a child of God. He is in control, and He will take care of you, if you let Him. Sunday is not the "catch-up" day, but a day to go to church, relax, have a leisurely dinner and then play catch with the kids.

Spend more time with the family, just enjoying each other's company in simple relaxed ways. Sunday is not the time to complain or discuss relationship problems. Be positive. Turn off the TV and iPhone and find the time to talk to each family member, heart-to-heart. Say: "I hear you," "Very interesting," "Tell me more." When we are rested, we have the energy to give our full attention to others.

REIGNITING THE INTIMACY

A woman was sipping a glass of wine, while sitting on the patio with her husband, and she says, "I love you so much, I don't know how I could ever live without you."
Her husband asks, "Is that you or the wine talking?"
She replies, "It's me...talking to the wine."

Intimacy at first comes spontaneously and passionately for a couple. But ask any exhausted pair of parents, and they can tell you that intimacy changes drastically after the first child. The fatigue is real. But that doesn't mean intimacy can't be reawakened.

Start with little gestures. Flowers are nature's perfume, artwork and jewelry. A flower's beauty is fleeting; it celebrates the precious present moment. Husbands should find any excuse to surprise their wife with flowers—especially in difficult days. It's easy to let loving signs slip after years of marriage. At first it may feel awkward, but do what it takes to bring them back to your relationship.

Affectionate touch always initiates an interaction. In a wedding, the couple join hands, exchange rings, kiss, and then embrace. Married couples should remain open to each other's embrace. They also have an obligation to their partners to keep their bodies, and figures, in good shape. Your body is a gift to your spouse; they might not want too big a gift!

Having a healthy sex life is of vital importance to any marriage. There are many factors which influence sexual intimacy: stress, worries, arguments, etc. The wife might be turned off by the husband's recent insensitive comments, or the husband may be resentful of nagging. The blame-game is not good for intimacy.

Proper communication can solve many of these issues. Each spouse should not be shy about communicating their own needs so that each spouse can fulfill their needs. Even if you are married many years, you may not necessarily be able to read each other's minds.

The sexual bonding may be influenced by unsuspected extraneous influences. As new parents, you will be tired most of the time and of course, that will affect your sexual desire. The husband may feel somewhat neglected when the newborn infant comes into the picture. The couple will still have needs for regular sexual activity, just as there remains a daily need for affection and words of love, praise and encouragement. These adjustments are quite essential during the beginnings of new parenthood, and the couple will find that their moods and desires will vary throughout married life.

In the ideal marriage, each spouse will always be very sensitive to their partner's needs. and not allow their own moods, whims or energy level to dictate the intimacy of their relationship.

The bedroom should be a haven where you escape from daily worries. It should be neat, clean, and relaxing. There should not be piles of papers, bills or magazines in view. No telephone calls accepted after a certain hour; let them leave a message. Avoid scrolling on social media.

We never thought it was wise to allow children to sleep in our bed or bedroom with us, only newborns. If children slept with us, it was impossible for us to have quality time together as a couple or get undisturbed sleep. Even we, the parents, tried to go to bed at a regular time, together.

These days, we joke that we have sixteen steps to bed: clothing in its place, dental care and flossing, skin care and lotion, sinuses, hair, nails, general hygiene, water, meds, muscle stretches, pillow and sheet adjustments, drapes, alarm clock settings, gospel reading, and examination of conscience. We must be careful not to take too long, or we may find our spouse fast asleep by the time we get to bed.

Bedtime ideally should be the time to give undivided attention to your spouse. The extra steps for a romantic evening: attractive nightwear, candles, scents, music, and perhaps a nightcap. If you are not feeling romantic, you can always be affectionate by holding hands, massaging the neck, or stroking hair or skin.

Outside of the bedroom, also make opportunities to be a couple. Have weekly dates and occasional weekend getaways where you can give undivided attention to each other, just relax, have fun and dream big together about all the things you have hoped for each other and your family, be that your next house, next child, next job, next trip, next project or next "mission."

SECTION V

HOW TO LIVE
"HAPPILY EVER AFTER"

Linas and I might sound like we have it all together, but we've had our fair share of challenges in our marriage. With such different personalities and approaches to certain problems, there were plenty of opportunities for misunderstandings and aggravation. We've gone a few days here and there without wanting to talk to or touch each other, like any normal couple, but we always try not to go to bed without reconciling.

Interestingly, even when we would go through a period of strain in our relationship, just by persevering, not giving up on each other, we were rewarded with the best of times.

We've also had several phases of financial stress, having such a big family to provide for, and having so many children to send off to college. Linas had to maintain three medical offices to support our family. Nevertheless, that did not stop him from going on annual medical missions to Lithuania for 20 years.

Linas was the first American intern to work in the USSR, in 1977, through the University of Chicago. He continued to teach eye implant surgery and bring in medical equipment when Lithuania regained its freedom in 1990.

Even though he had full support from me to dedicate so much time, money and effort in the land of our ancestors, it was not easy being without a husband and father around the house for several weeks of the year. In 2008, he was knighted by the President of Lithuania for his many contributions to medicine in Lithuania.

Fortunately, we and our children were of good health and none had major behavioral problems, but there were always issues to solve.

No matter what was going on in our family, good or bad, one of the things that kept Linas and me cheerful were the many times we were able to dance together throughout the years! This was one way we could have fun and feel young again.

As parents, one of the greatest gifts you can give your children is a loving relationship with one other.

COMMUNICATE WITH CARE

It was their three-month wedding anniversary, and as the young couple drove along, the recent bride couldn't restrain her emotions: "I can't believe it's been a whole three months! It's incredible how quickly time flies..." The young man nodded in agreement and added: "Yup, three months. It's time for an oil change."

Most arguments could be avoided if we just listened to what our spouse is saying: really saying. "He who has ears to hear, let him hear!" Matt. 11:15. Frequently your verbal response is secondary to the message that your attention is sending: "I care about you and what you are feeling."

Of course the timing, the content and the place of the conversation is important. Don't try to have a meaningful conversation with a hungry person. The classical phrase is: "the way to a man's heart is through his stomach," not, "the way to a man's heart is through his ears." In many cases, don't even try to engage a person before they have had their morning cup of coffee. Remember, don't raise issues when someone is cooking, changing diapers, preoccupied with the kids, or racing to get to work.

Couples must frequently remember that finding the right time to talk things out is of utmost importance. This is the time when men must learn and practice audible responses such as: "I hear you", "I agree, this sounds important..." A grunt in response to a question is understood by other men, but it doesn't typically cut it for women.

In a heart-to-heart talk, the other person feels the need to feel they are being understood and appreciated. Not every serious talk involves a problem to be addressed and a resolution to be found.

The male spouse will get frustrated when there is an issue raised that he does not quite understand and does not know how to solve. He wants to problem solve, rather than simply listen. As his wife seeks to explain issues by talking about problems, she does not realize how much stress she may be inducing in her husband.

If a husband does not see the conversation leading to something he must do, a situation he should solve or advice he can offer, he thinks talking is useless and a waste of time. He has left his work and the day's problems at the office, and planned to relax at home. And now his wife is giving him more work to do: or is she? It may be that she has already resolved the issue in her own mind, and just wanted to explain how she came to her conclusion. It takes a while for him to figure it out. He may not understand and so not answer immediately. His wife may think he is not listening to her.

Many men think like Abraham Lincoln who quipped, "Better to remain silent and be thought a fool, than to speak out and remove all doubt."

These days work situations vary. The man is not necessarily the "bread winner" and the mother is not necessarily staying at home with the kids. Whatever the situation, it is critical that you continually place yourself in your spouse's shoes. You should try your best to understand what their day has been like, so you can empathize with them, communicate well, and attend to their needs.

If the wife is a full-time housewife, she doesn't physically leave her work. Her home is her workplace. These transitions take place in one space: from housewife, to home manager, to mother, to wife, to best friend and then romantic companion! This is not emotionally easy. The transitions are facilitated by talking about the day, sharing thoughts and reactions, setting a new tone and getting into the new role. This transition requires attentive listening by the husband: undivided attention, without the newspaper, TV or smartphone.

We had a more traditional model of marriage where I as the husband took care of the finances and big picture problems. Rima tackled the details of daily life and the children's immediate needs. She primarily took care of the house and its maintenance, I would mostly work outside in the yard. All of those roles are important.

When the work load at home became too much, for several years we hired house cleaners and day-time nannies.

These days, you will find many different variations from the traditional family. Two incomes are often needed, and in cases where the mother's income is greater, you have stay-at-home Dads. These situations are definitely doable in the short-term, but there might be more ideal situations for the long-term. Most men will admit that it is very difficult to spend the entire day taking care of children. Do whatever works for you as a couple and is best for the kids. Be flexible and communicate clearly your preferences.

KEEP FINANCES IN CHECK

"Where your treasure is, there your heart will be also." - Matt. 6:21

Finances are one of the main areas of disagreements in marriage and a major factor in divorces. The attitude that this money is "my" money, the rest is "our" money, leads to trouble. If two become "one body," then logically, the two bank accounts and the debts also become one: a joint account.

Which is more important, your body or your money? If you are freely giving your body to your spouse, then you should also give your money and your future earnings to your spouse and children.

The Scriptures say: "the love of money is the root of all evils" 1 Tim. 6:10. The American mentality is more like: "Lack of money is the root of all evil." Money is not evil in itself, but it can become evil when too much importance is given to it. It is quite surprising that in the Gospels, in 11 out of 39 parables Jesus talks about money. He examines both the good and bad use of money, most vividly in the parable of the "talents" in Matt. 25:14-30.

Excessive educational debts these days can be a real shocker to your spouse after marriage. Full disclosure should be made before getting married. Parents should also consider, is it worth sending your child to that prestigious, but very expensive college?

Attitudes vary greatly. Some people are insecure and for them, saving money is future security. Our society pushes the idea that one's "net worth" is equal to one's actual worth: the proof of their importance. An insecure person believes this. For others, spending money gives them an emotional high, an affirmation of their own success. Some want to accumulate, others want to experience. Some become misers, others spendthrifts. Both attitudes become problems, financial and moral. These stem from selfishness and materialism, when one's wants become needs. We need to learn the virtues of temperance and detachment from money and material things. Couples need to align their financial expectations with each other. Otherwise, there will be trouble, and a personal "recession" or "depression." Some tips to consider:

1. Make the financial decisions together. You will learn a lot about each other in this process. This requires transparency and communication.

2. Start saving for the future: even if only 1% of your earnings at the beginning. We strongly suggest starting a tax-free Roth IRA. It is amazing how your wealth will exponentially grow when you start investing tax-free early in your marriage.

3. Make a budget. Work the budget, and make it work. Separate the frivolous from the essential. Have a six-month financial cushion available for emergencies.

4. If yours is a one-income family, the one who earns the income should have life-insurance coverage.

5. Learn as much as you can about the tax laws that apply to your income and estate. Save and store all of the tax reports, investment and interest income info, 1099's, for six years.

6. Discuss charitable giving. This is an obligation for everyone who earns money. When, how much, to what charities? If the budget is very limited, people can give their time and volunteer.

7. Talk to parents of large families in your community who seem to be doing a good job raising their kids and managing finances. They will have plenty of good advice: swapping children's clothing and toys with friends, or shopping at thrift stores, which our teenagers loved to do.

8. Preparing for, and providing for children should be a priority. However, a future expense such as college tuition is not a valid reason for limiting your family. Not everyone wants or needs to go to college. Many college grads end up working in jobs which do not require a college degree. Teach the children, at an early age, to earn their money by doing chores: helping neighbors with yard work, babysitting…

9. Buy good quality items and make them last. That bookshelf you bought as newlyweds could become a family heirloom, so buy a nice one. Hand out good books you have read to others; will you really find time to reread them?

10. Caution: pets can be very expensive! A large drain on time and money but they're very good for companionship and teaching kids responsibility. You can always start with a fish or hamster, if not looking for serious pet management.

11. Kids have too many toys these days. Put a limit on toys the kids can access any given day. Ask the grandparents not to gift toys, but rather send gift cards, or spend money for an outing.

12. Don't give in to the "Fast Fashion" fads, and stick with quality pieces of clothing. Clean out your closets regularly. T-shirts and sweatshirts mysteriously multiply in closets.

13. Expensive hotels don't include breakfast, whereas economy hotels do. Also, small kids can sleep on the sofa or on the floor. Just bring that extra pillow and blanket.

14. Regular use of coupons for food shopping teaches your children how to be frugal, especially when Dad leads the way and does it himself. Clipping and sorting coupons was a family activity, even for little kids.

15. Research credit cards and know all the perks they offer. Look for banks or brokerage companies that don't charge fees.

16. Always check bills, receipts and credit card statements for mistakes. If the offer seems too good to be true, it probably is. Be on your guard. Beware of those telephone marketers.

17. Do not give your children the latest gadgets as soon as they come out. Make them wait or even earn them. Our kids were often the last ones to get the latest video game or toy, if at all; and we did it on purpose. Even one of our girls asked her father one day, "Are we rich or poor?" It is good to keep them guessing. Our son once said: "If you don't have money to buy this toy for me, let's go to the bank, they always have money!"

18. When you start having children, make a Will. When you get older and accumulate wealth, make a Living Trust.

19. Remember: "In God we trust." There is a rumor that our heavily indebted government is planning to remove "In God we trust" from our currency and change it to: "God help us!" Manage your debt so that doesn't become your family motto.

DON'T NEGLECT YOUR SEX LIFE

"Conjugal love is an 'affective union,' spiritual and sacrificial, which combines the warmth of friendship and erotic passion, and endures long after emotions and passions subside." - Pope Francis, Amoris Laetitia

My philosophy professor at Notre Dame used to say in the classroom: "Sex is easy; you can do it lying down!"

So, why does sex get neglected in married life? Why might one partner hold back when another initiates? What is missing in what should be a mutually wonderful bonding experience?

As a physician, I am of the opinion that for men sex is a stress-reliever. For women, it's often a stress-inducer. Men tend to want sex anytime, since it makes them feel good and makes them forget their problems. In contrast, women need to feel good, forget their problems and "get in the mood" before they have sex. A man can be tired, sick, hungry, angry or all of the above, and yet he can still be ready for sex. For a woman, any one of those conditions will likely make sex the last thing on her mind.

Men are straightforward; they are quickly physically aroused and then quickly satisfied. For a woman, the sexual act is much more complicated, both physically and emotionally, due to her menstrual cycles, pregnancy, postpartum phases, menopause, or even her body image. In general, women are slower to become aroused, and very often the setting or her mood has to be just right. For these reasons, the woman can end up less satisfied with the outcome of the sexual encounter.

Ideally, both partners should find pleasure and satisfaction in the sexual encounter, but this is not always the case. The wife should also experience orgasms in sexual activity, but this often will take extra patience, effort and understanding on the man's part.

In "Love and Responsibility," Pope John Paul II writes: "It must be taken into account that it is naturally difficult for the woman to adapt herself to the man in the sexual relationship, that there is a natural unevenness of the physical and psychological rhythms, so that there is a need for harmonization, which is impossible without goodwill, especially on the part of the man, who must carefully observe the reactions of the woman. If a woman does not obtain natural gratification from the sexual act there is a danger that her experience of it will be qualitatively inferior, and will not involve her fully as a person."

A woman wants to feel that her man is genuinely interested in her as a person. That means a man must be attentive to her outside of the bedroom and inside the bedroom. She wants to remain a person, not just a body. She wants to know that she is beautiful and desirable, but above-all cherished for her personal qualities. She wants her husband to understand that she has her own particular sexuality which he must discover and tend to. Both men and women must realize that sexuality is not just physical, but it "concerns the innermost being of the human person" - Pope John Paul II.

Sometimes the solution to problems of mutual satisfaction may be as simple as using baby oil to alleviate discomfort, but more often than not, we need to communicate clearly what we want or don't want from each other sexually. For others, there can be an underlying physical or psychological problem requiring professional help.

Some people may have inhibitions about sex due to the fact that they grew up thinking that sex is "dirty." Others had negative or illicit sexual encounters in their past.

Growing up in the Catholic faith, the emphasis was on the moral prohibition of sex *outside* of marriage, rather than focusing on sexuality *in* marriage. For people who are looking for more clarity into recent Catholic teachings, we recommend Christopher West's book, "Good News About Sex & Marriage." He is a popular speaker and writer, a husband and father. In a question/answer format he explains the deeper meaning of human sexuality according to God's plan for marriage and the practical aspects of living our sexuality in daily life as presented in Pope John Paul II's "Theology of the Body."

In general, spouses should try to become fully available to each other sexually and emotionally as much as possible, since this is what marriage is about—trying our best to fulfill the legitimate needs and desires of each other. By being attentive to our spouse, we help them to avoid falling for temptations. We are not saying that you are responsible for the sins of your spouse, but that you can definitely help your spouse stay faithful to the marriage vows.

Faithfulness to your spouse requires what traditionally was called "custody of the heart." Unfortunately, if couples fail to tend to the other's needs, some will become unhappy with their spouse. This negligence will make them more vulnerable to temptations. It will be used as an excuse to have extramarital affairs or to view pornography. Couples who socialize too closely with other couples, or people in their workplace who become too familiar with co-workers also run the risk of serious temptations.

When a person is neglected or bored, they may then try to feed their fantasies with magazines, steamy romance novels, indecent movies or porn. This is not the way to spice up your love life; it is like inviting someone else into your bedroom.

As couples mature, the sexual aspect may diminish in frequency, but the importance of touch will never diminish. No matter whether you are exhausted or just "not in the mood" you can and should stay physically close, whether it is by giving your spouse a mini-massage, stroking their skin or just holding hands at the end of the day. Even these little things are needed in lasting love.

KISS AND MAKE UP!

"Don't end the day without making peace. To make peace, it's not necessary to call the UN. A small gesture is enough, a caress, for example. Then, move on and wake up the next day and start again." - Pope Francis, Amoris Laetitia *(The Joy of Love)*

The immediate need during an argument is to calm down and negotiate a settlement. Do not go to bed angry. The comic actress Imogene Coca offered somewhat different advice: "Do not go to bed angry," Coca advised, "Keep on fighting!" That is the choice. The other partner may not agree with your offer of a truce.

The spouses must realize, deep down, that both parties in any argument are at fault. Issues are so wrapped together, at so many intellectual and emotional levels, that neither party is ever totally innocent. Furthermore, who appointed you the prosecutor, or the jury, or the judge? Be humble. The important thing is not to win the argument but to win back the peace.

In fact, you cannot win. In fighting your spouse, you are fighting yourself, for you are one flesh, one body. Sometimes angry young children try to demonstrate to their parents what terrible things their sibling has done to them by hitting themselves, pulling their own hair, repeating those demeaning insults. Don't be childish. Don't beat up on yourself: calm down, negotiate a settlement and let your spouse save face. Develop some personal signs that you are willing to compromise, to de-escalate the conflict.

There are important guidelines to follow in nuptial argument to avoid escalation and to avoid inflicting permanent wounds in the psyche.

Do not expect your spouse to suddenly stop arguing and say: "You're right, I'm wrong. You've convinced me. I will now kneel before you and kiss your foot, and never argue with you again because you are so superior to me."

Totally unreasonable expectations. Just take a breath to calm down. The odds are, the next day, or in a couple days, this argument will be forgotten. As it should be. In a Catholic marriage, leave the judging to God. If the spouse goes to Confession; let the priest evaluate the situation. In the loving spirit of Christ, the priest will give advice, penance and forgiveness. Reconciliation, with God, and your spouse, is always possible. For Catholics, divorce is not an option or the answer!

Without the graces offered in the Sacrament of Reconciliation (Confession), the union may be gravely wounded and scarred by emotional arguments and insults. Without forgiveness (of oneself and of the other), a lot of anger and resentment can fester. The couple might co-exists in misery for a while, and may need to go to therapy or counseling, or they may end up in the divorce court. We see this over and over again.

But divorce doesn't really solve the problem. Talking to people who have gone through it, you will often find the inner pain of the broken marriage has never fully healed. The betrayal, hypocrisy and selfishness involved leave a great void, a great pain, and a great sadness, indeed. For the children, divorce is a trauma. It will affect their self-esteem, religious faith, and their future relationships.

If anyone you know is contemplating divorce, have them read "Primal Loss, The Now-Adult Children of Divorce Speak," by Leila Miller. It will make anyone think twice about the lifelong suffering divorce brings upon their children. It dispels the myth that their children "will get over it."

Some Considerations for Resolving Arguments:

1. Recognize that both of you are to blame for arguing; perhaps one more than the other, but both share the blame.

2. Both will eventually need to apologize to each other. So, leave an opening for a reconciliation.

3. Do your best to resolve the issue. At least try to come to a partial mutual understanding.

4. Do not wound, do not say anything that will leave permanent emotional scars that you will regret later.

5. Throwing things, threats and physical touch is totally off limits. Stop! Communication is over for now. Come back later, when you cool down.

6. The person who gives in first and is more conciliatory, less stubborn and more forgiving, is actually more loving.

7. Get over the "martyr complex." The humble martyrs died for Christ, who died for us. You are wounded by your own personal pride, anger and stubbornness.

8. In an argument, men will never fully understand women's reasoning; and vice-versa. Try to be charitable and find the points you agree with.

9. Each think differently. Women's issues are complex, dynamic, and very interconnected. By contrast, men compartmentalize issues. Each subject has its own, separate

place, like an App on a cell phone. Men's favorite place is the "Nothing Box", like when he goes fishing, does not think about anything, just stares into the water... See the hilarious YouTube video, "Laugh Your Way to a Better Marriage," by Mark Gungor.

10. A long, drawn-out heated argument, and the sullen, silent aftermath, is physically tiring, emotionally draining and a total waste of time. Be smart: hug and make up.

11. The argument will be resolved eventually. Don't be "MAD." In military terms, MAD, mutually assured destruction which threatened total atomic war, but eventually resulted in peace treaties and disarmament.

12. Misunderstandings and arguments are part of a normal marriage. However, frequent arguments and very heated discussions are not normal. This couple needs professional counseling to resolve recurrent issues and deeper problems.

The Rules of Engagement:

1. When angry, do not argue right away. Agree to 20 minutes to one hour alone to cool off, then come back together to discuss the issue. Of course, never argue in front of the kids.

2. Do not argue after 10:00 pm and don't argue in the bedroom.

3. Set a limit to the length of the argument, say, one hour. If there is more to say, agree to a truce, and continue the discussion later.

4. If you have been drinking, don't argue until both parties are sober. If one person is drunk, the other should just listen patiently, to avoid unnecessary escalation.

5. Make sure each person is arguing about the same issue. Discuss just one issue at a time.

6. Don't raise your voice or shout. Don't cut the other one off. Avoid cursing or staring: staring can be a hostile action. Be aware of your body language. Do not cross your arms. Don't quote mother-in-laws. They aren't authorities in your marriage, so don't quote them.

7. Keep it current. Do not bring up what the other supposedly said months ago.

8. Do not make general, sweeping statements: "You are hopeless." "You never listen." "You're always stubborn."

9. Avoid cynicism: "And you think you are a good person!" "Why did I ever marry you?" "Men are all alike!" "Why can't a woman be more like a man?" Recently, we have used "And you wrote a book on marriage?!"

10. Do not quote the Bible to support your arguments. Leave Jesus out of your petty fight and God out of your expletives.

11. If all else fails, have a snack or prepare a sandwich. In couples therapy, they recommend never starting a serious discussion while drunk, hungry or tired.

12. Civilized warfare honors the white flag, indicating a truce. Arrange your own personal truce signal. Turn towards each other, give an unexpected hug or a soft and kind word.

LIVING WITH TRAGEDY TOGETHER

"If a family is centered on Christ, he will unify and illuminate its entire life. Moments of pain and difficulty will be experienced in union with the Lord's cross, and his closeness will make it possible to surmount them." - Pope Francis, Amoris Laetitia (The Joy of Love)

In 2009 our family was hit with a sudden tragedy. Our fifth child, Saule, died at the age of 23. For loving parents, this was unimaginable. Saule was known and loved by many for being easy-going, cheerful, gentle, quirky, poetic and philosophical. She was known for her "sunny" smile, as her name means "sun" in Lithuanian. She loved to dance and sing with all her heart. She was the one who would give her utmost attention to the loneliest person in the room or a homeless person on the street. She also liked to promote the idea of doing "random acts of kindness."

Losing her was something too painful to accurately put into words, but we didn't let the grief consume us. We relied on our closeness as a family, we communicated openly with each other, tried to understand what everyone was going through, and we showed each other genuine affection.

We prayed the Rosary individually and as a family, went to Mass together and talked to our priests, relatives, friends and spiritual advisers. We shared our thoughts, memories and feelings about Saule, her life and her death, about death itself, and even maintained a loving sense of humor about things that were unique to her.

Most often after the death of a child, the parents feel like life will never be the same, and their own lives seem doomed to be gray and joyless. One tends to relive the tragedy over and over again, until

104

your own life feels like a never-ending tragedy. Often the spouses start irrationally blaming one another for the child's death, or they feel guilt-ridden that they could have, or should have, done more to prevent the death of their child. Such couples may even eventually divorce. They lose their faith in God. They cannot understand why a loving God would allow such a horrible thing, especially when the person who dies is so young. Nevertheless, my husband and I kept reminding ourselves and our children, "Even though our family experienced a tragedy, our lives are not tragic."

Families who have Faith and live an active prayer life are accustomed to seeing God's Will in all things—even the hardest ones to fathom. They realize that life and death come from the hands of God. There are no accidents, there is only His Providence. We know that God can draw great good out of what appears to be evil or unfortunate, even though we don't see the good at the time.

We actually saw many good and beautiful things that came out of Saule's death. We saw the love people had for her and our family. We saw people reevaluating their lives and appreciating their loved ones more. We saw people praying more, and some even found their Faith again. We are certain that there were many more hidden and wondrous things that we will only find out about in the next life.

We are so grateful to God that he gave us eight wonderful children. He gave us Saule for 23 years, and he took her back to Himself precisely when He willed it so. We believe in the resurrection of the body. We truly believe that we will see each other again, after we complete this very brief life's journey on Earth towards Heaven.

"God is like a gardener who cares for the flowers: he waters them, he protects them, and he only cuts them when they are most beautiful and full of richness." - St. Josemaria Escriva.

KEEP THE ROMANCE ALIVE

"If a happy marriage is like a hearth burning with love, lively and beautiful, giving light and warmth to all, then romance is the kindling that begins the fire and keeps it going." - Rima Sidrys

Our adult children, most of whom are married, often ask us to explain what it takes to have a joyful marriage. How do we keep things interesting after so many years together, especially after raising so many children? We might not have all the answers, but we are certain, that in spite of all the doubt and skepticism revolving marriage these days, every person has a deep desire to find lasting love. It begins with the little things. Here are our tips that have stood the test of time.

1. Throughout our marriage we continued to do the activity that brought us together in the first place—dancing. We have danced countless times together and only with each other, and we still love all kinds of dancing with the same enthusiasm as in the early days. A couple should do things that remind them of when they first fell in love. If you both met while skiing, jogging or singing, continue to do so after marriage, perhaps with your children.

2. Every now and then do something together that neither had done before. As newlyweds we edited a magazine. Now, we are writing a book together. We love stimulating conversation, so for seven years we hosted family discussion groups in our home. Traveling is always exciting, because you are constantly discovering new things. Think "out of the box":

help others, even strangers, in need. When Lithuania was struggling for independence from the Soviet Union, we aided them with medicine, money, visits, political protests, smuggling in religious literature, hosting dozens of visitors from newly independent Lithuania in our home. By helping and serving others, there was never a dull moment in our family!

3. Every single day, you should do or say something to your spouse that shows you love them—even if you don't feel like it. This advice was given at every family wedding from Linas' father of nine children. Every day do little things that make the other appreciated, no matter how small or brief: a smile, a compliment, a hug, a kiss, a rose, a little service, undivided attention, time spent together, a walk, a heartfelt thank you.

4. "Wives should take good care of their appearance as they did before they were married, and husbands should show the same affection as a young man who has just fallen in love." - St. Josemaria Escriva. As old-fashioned as that sounds, we really lived by this, and we both tried not to let ourselves go. Try your best to do what your spouse finds attractive. Even in a house with many children, I made a huge effort to dress nicely and put makeup on every day, so I would look pretty for my husband and children. My husband has always stayed fit by running, walking or swimming. On weekends, we often had fun getting dressed up and dancing together at weddings, banquets, and other social events.

5. Take an interest in each other's interests. If your husband likes football, try to take an interest in football, or at least pretend you're interested. Go with him to a game at least once a year. At the very least, give him good snacks for his TV football games and sit for part of the game. If your wife likes classical concerts and you would rather listen to country, take her to that expensive classical concert! And don't be a bad sport about it! Remember, true love is in the will, not just doing things when you feel like it.

6. Go on a weekly date no matter what. It's worthwhile. This was the best marriage advice I ever got! I was given this advice by a holy priest, in the confessional. I told him that with four small children, I used to feel anything but affectionate at the end of the day. I felt like a beat up horse, just work, work, work, while kids interrupted me all day long, shouting: "Mama, Mama!" He advised me to go on a date with my husband every week. I asked the priest if we should discuss the children on our date, and he retorted "No, be a romantic couple again!" We went to a pub for our "first date." It felt so strange, I did not know what to do with my hands, since I wasn't holding a baby bottle or scrambling after a frisky toddler. Look into each other's eyes, hold hands, kiss, etc. There were days we were so tired, our "date" was going for a walk around the block, while our children slept.

7. Go on weekend getaways each season. Back in the 1980's when we had five young children, we noticed ads about bargain weekend getaways at classy hotels. After enlisting a series of babysitters, and packing light, we escaped with minimum fuss. Even though it was only 30 minutes away, we felt like we really "got away from it all!" For a couple of nights, we relaxed, swam, had great discussions, went to restaurants, and came back refreshed.

8. Go on separate Retreats every year. It's healthy to detach oneself for a few days from spouse, children, everyday work and worries in a quiet, restful environment. This is a spiritual "adventure." There we place everything trustingly in God's hands, including everyone you left behind. Not only will you be spiritually and physically renewed, but you'll also be greatly missed by your spouse and children and feel loved all the more upon your return. Remember, that "distance makes the heart grow fonder."

9. Confession regularly, at least once a month, makes us spiritually fit. We get rid of a lot of "baggage" when we own up to our sins and are forgiven by God, through the priest. Even when we find that we keep repeating the same defects, we develop the mother of all virtues, "humility." Genuine humility also makes us accept others just as they are, and we are more sympathetic to their weaknesses. We don't judge others as readily and are more patient with them, since we see our own limitations so clearly. By confessing regularly, we cleanse ourselves of spiritual toxins in our souls that make us dirty, heavy, and tired. It is a Fountain of Youth.

- - -

You will notice that all of these tips are designed to heighten your sense of togetherness. They work for the two of us, but surely each couple will have their own preferences. Be creative and whatever you decide to do—do it with style!

EPILOGUE

And so, our journey has taken us to this moment in time. We've raised eight children who all grew up to be interesting, intelligent and good-hearted adults. Each one has chosen a vastly different field of work from the first to the last: Human Rights Advocacy, Finance, Speech Pathology, Tech Program Management, Education, Dentistry, Military Aviation, and the Arts. Scattered across all of America, our children and their talented, family-loving spouses welcome us to their corner of the country—and we can entertain and be entertained by our 16 grandchildren who are still so small, yet so full of big personalities.

There is never a dull moment with a big Catholic family like ours. The sacrifices that once seemed so insurmountable to us, look so small in hindsight. We thank God for all of it. Each phase of life brings its own set of difficulties, but then new graces abound.

The teachings of the Catholic Church include some of the highest ideals, that often seem humanly impossible to keep. Luckily, it isn't based solely on human effort. What's important is that we aim high, and keep our eyes set on Christ, our Savior. Without Him it will be impossible because humanly speaking, the demands of life, and especially of married life, will prove to be too much.

"Nunc Coepi!" is the Latin phrase meaning "now I begin." The Christian life is all about Christ, and when we fall short of following in His footsteps, we simply begin again, and again, and again... This is the path to Heaven. It is paved with struggle and suffering, but it is also filled with family and friends who help us along the way.

We hope this book helped you see more clearly the great mission God has set out for you and your spouse. He wants you to be able to love each other more purely, more selflessly and more passionately than you can ever imagine. He has high hopes for you, and so do we. You will be in our prayers. Go live out your greatest adventure! With God, all things are possible...

PHOTO CAPTIONS

Front Cover: Honeymoon, Acapulco, "Our First Selfie," April 1978

Rima's Story: Lithuanian Folk Dance Festival, Chicago, 1976, p. 4

Linas' Story: Graduation from University of Chicago, Pritzker School of Medicine, Chicago, 1977, p. 8

Section I: Honeymoon, Acapulco, April 1978, p. 12

Section II: Engagement, Chicago, 1977, p. 30

Section III: Wedding photo, Chicago, April 1978, p. 56

Section IV: Our first two children, Gainesville, FL, 1981, p. 70

Section V: Family Portrait (Back row from left: Lina, Rimas, Vija. Front row from left: Vincas, Gaja, **Linas,** Ziba, **Rima**, Saule, and Gintas), Chicago, 1997, p. 86

Epilogue: Family Christmas 2016, "Twenty-Four Souls Living Under One Roof for Ten Days," Palos Hills, IL, p. 112

Our Fifteen Grandchildren, Christmas 2018, Palos Hills, IL, p. 114

After 41 Years of Marriage, 2019, Palos Hills, IL, p. 116

Made in USA - Crawfordsville, IN
47875_9798601890465
04.01.2022 1658